펼쳐 보면 느껴집니다

단 한 줄도 배움의 공백이 생기지 않도록
문장 한 줄마다 20년이 넘는
해커스의 영어교육 노하우를 담았음을

덮고 나면 확신합니다

수많은 선생님의 목소리와
정확한 출제 데이터 분석으로 꽉 찬
교재 한 권이면 충분함을

해커스북 중·고등
HackersBook.com

WHY
HACKERS
READING SMART?

FUN & INFORMATIVE

**최신 이슈가 반영된
흥미롭고 유익한**

독해 지문

**배경지식이
풍부해지는**

Read & Learn

**재미있는 활동과
읽을거리가 가득한**

FUN FUN한 BREAK

**Hackers
Reading Smart**

Level 1

**Hackers
Reading Smart**

Level 2

**Hackers
Reading Smart**

Level 3

**Hackers
Reading Smart**

Level 4

SMART & EFFECTIVE

**최신 출제 경향을
철저히 반영한**

다양한 유형의 문제

**본책을 그대로 담은
편리하고 친절한**

해설집

**추가 연습문제로
독해 실력을 완성하는**

WORKBOOK

HACKERS
READING SMART

LEVEL 3

HACKERS

Contents

HACKERS READING SMART LEVEL 3

Overview

Fun & Informative

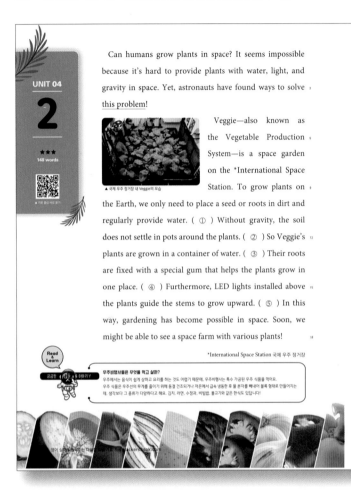

Can humans grow plants in space? It seems impossible because it's hard to provide plants with water, light, and gravity in space. Yet, astronauts have found ways to solve this problem!

Veggie—also known as the Vegetable Production System—is a space garden on the *International Space Station. To grow plants on the Earth, we only need to place a seed or roots in dirt and regularly provide water. (①) Without gravity, the soil does not settle in pots around the plants. (②) So Veggie's plants are grown in a container of water. (③) Their roots are fixed with a special gum that helps the plants grow in one place. (④) Furthermore, LED lights installed above the plants guide the stems to grow upward. (⑤) In this way, gardening has become possible in space. Soon, we might be able to see a space farm with various plants!

*International Space Station 국제 우주 정거장

▲ 국제 우주 정거장 내 Veggie의 모습

우주비행사들은 무엇을 먹고 살까?
우주에서는 음식이 쉽게 상하고 요리를 하는 것도 어렵기 때문에, 우주비행사는 특수 가공된 우주 식품을 먹어요. 우주 식품은 우주선의 무게를 줄이기 위해 동결 건조되거나 저온에서 금속 냉동한 후 물 분자를 빼내어 블록 형태로 만들어지는데, 생각보다 그 종류가 다양하다고 해요. 김치, 라면, 수정과, 비빔밥, 불고기와 같은 한식도 있답니다!

UNIT 04

2

★★★
148 words

1. 이 글의 제목을 다음과 같이 나타낼 때, 빈칸에 들어갈 말을 글에서 찾아 쓰시오. (단, 주어진 철자로 시작하여 쓰시오.)

Growing P _____ in a S _____ Garden Called Veggie

〔서술형〕
2. 이 글의 밑줄 친 this problem이 의미하는 내용을 우리말로 쓰시오.

_____

3. 이 글의 흐름으로 보아, 다음 문장이 들어가기에 가장 적절한 곳은?

However, this doesn't work in space.

①   ②   ③   ④   ⑤

4. Veggie의 구성 요소와 각각의 역할을 알맞게 연결하시오.

(A) a water container •   • (1) to prevent the roots from moving
(B) a special gum •   • (2) to replace the soil in zero gravity
(C) LED lights •   • (3) to help the stems grow upward

5. 이 글의 내용으로 보아, 다음 빈칸에 들어갈 말을 보기에서 골라 쓰시오.

보기   gardening   natural   landing   farm   artificial

Recently, astronauts have invented a new _____ method that uses water, gum, and _____ lights to grow plants in the conditions of space. One day, we may even run a space _____.

Words
provide A with B A에게 B를 제공하다 gravity 圈중력 astronaut 圈우주 비행사 production 圈생산 seed 圈씨앗 root 圈뿌리 dirt 圈흙 regularly 圈주기적으로 soil 圈흙 settle 圈고정되다; (눈물을) 재결하다 pot 圈화분 container 圈용기, 그릇 fix 圈고정시키다; 수리하다 gum 圈고무 install 圈설치하다 stem 圈줄기 upward 圈위로 gardening 圈원예
<문제> work 圈잘되다, 유효하게 작용하다; 일하다 replace 圈대체하다 artificial 圈인공의, 인공적인 conditions 圈환경; (단수형) 상태; 조건 run 圈운영하다

UNIT 04 | 47

---

1. 흥미롭고 유익한 지문

최신 이슈와 관심사 반영
국내외 다양한 최신 이슈와 관심사가 반영된 흥미진진한 지문으로 재미있게 독해 실력을 쌓을 수 있어요.

교과서 연계 소재 반영
과학, 문화, 예술 등 교과서와 연계되는 최신 소재의 지문이 담겨 있어, 중등 교과 과정에 대한 이해력을 높일 수 있어요.

2. 배경지식이 풍부해지는 Read & Learn

지문과 관련된 유용한 배경지식을 읽으며, 지문 내용에 대해 확실히 이해하고 상식도 넓힐 수 있어요.

3. 추리 지문으로 독해력 up 재미도 up!

범인은 이 안에 있다! 교재의 마지막 지문에서는 추리 퀴즈를 다루고 있어요. 상상력과 추리력을 발휘해서 퀴즈를 풀어보며 재미있게 독해 실력을 키울 수 있어요.

4. 재미있는 활동과 읽을거리가 가득한 Fun Fun한 Break

각 UNIT의 마지막 페이지에는 지문과 관련된 다양한 활동과 읽을거리가 담겨 있어, 재미있게 학습을 마무리할 수 있어요.

Smart & Effective

1. 효과적으로 독해 실력을 향상시키는
다양한 유형의 문제

서술형 문제
다양한 유형의 서술형 문제로 학교 내신 시험에도 대비할 수 있어요.

심화형 문제
조금 더 어려운 심화형 문제로 사고력을 키우고 독해 실력을 향상시킬 수 있어요.

다양한 도표 문제
표, 전개도 등 지문 내용을 도식화한 다양한 유형의 문제로 글의 구조와 핵심을 파악하는 능력을 키울 수 있어요.

English Only
각 UNIT의 마지막 지문에서는 영어로만 구성되어 있는 문제를 읽고 풀며 영어 실력을 더욱 강화할 수 있어요.

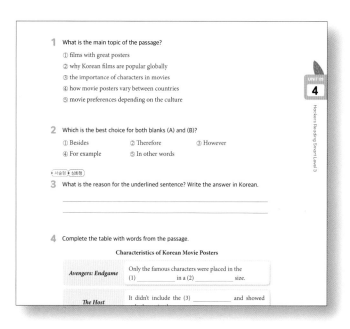

2. 추가 연습문제로 독해 실력을 완성하는 워크북

직독직해 워크시트
각 지문에 대한 직독직해와 문장별 주어·동사를 파악하는 훈련을 통해 한 문장씩 완벽히 복습할 수 있어요.

서술형 추가 문제
어휘·구문 확인 문제와 다양한 유형의 추가 서술형 문제를 통해 지문 내용을 확실히 익히고 영작 실력도 키울 수 있어요.

3. 본책을 그대로 담은 편리하고 친절한 해설집

본책의 지문과 문제를 그대로 담아 편리하게 학습할 수 있어요. 문장의 정확한 해석을 알려주는 직독직해와 본문 해석, 오답의 이유까지 설명해주는 자세한 문제 해설, 예문과 함께 제공되는 친절한 구문 해설을 통해 꼼꼼히 복습할 수 있어요.

HackersBook.com

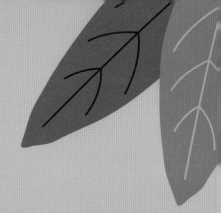

UNIT 01

Imagine someone has been rushed to the hospital after a car accident. The patient starts losing a lot of blood during an operation. The hospital asks the supply center for more blood. (①) But it can take hours to deliver blood bags by car. (②) It only takes 15 minutes to deliver the bags! (③) Drones have already made life-saving deliveries like this 25,000 times in Africa alone. (④) And they make the deliveries without landing. (⑤) The drones simply drop a box containing medical supplies from the sky. The box is attached to a small parachute, which allows it to land safely.

However, this isn't the only task drones perform to save lives. They play an especially big role when _____ after natural disasters. Drones can search in the dark or in areas that are hard to reach. So a drone is sometimes the best way to save people in need of rescue.

Read & Learn

도와줘요, 꿀벌 드론!

전 세계적으로 꿀벌의 수가 급격히 감소하면서 지구 생태계가 위험에 처해 있는데, 이 문제를 드론이 해결할 수 있을지도 몰라요. 꿀벌은 세계 식량 자원의 70% 이상을 만들어 내는 작물의 수분을 돕는 역할을 해서, 꿀벌의 멸종은 큰 위기를 불러올 것이라고 해요. 이에 대비해 꿀벌을 대신할 수 있는 새로운 드론이 만들어졌답니다. 작은 몸체를 가진 이 드론은 진짜 꿀벌처럼 꽃가루를 옮겨 꽃과 나무의 수분을 도울 수 있다고 해요.

1 이 글의 제목으로 가장 적절한 것은?

① Accidents Caused by Drones

② Is Delivery by Drones Possible?

③ How Drones Will Affect the Future

④ The Need for Medical Support in Africa

⑤ The Use of Drones to Help People in Danger

2 이 글의 흐름으로 보아, 다음 문장이 들어가기에 가장 적절한 곳은?

> Instead, the center sends a drone.

① ② ③ ④ ⑤

3 이 글의 빈칸에 들어갈 말로 가장 적절한 것은?

① delivering food to people

② looking for missing people

③ checking people's health

④ offering free medical care

⑤ repairing some damaged buildings

4 이 글의 내용으로 보아, 다음 빈칸에 공통으로 들어갈 말을 글에서 찾아 쓰시오.

> Drones can _____ time when delivering medical supplies in an emergency. They can also be used to _____ people's lives in disaster areas.

Words

rush 图 급히 수송하다   accident 图 사고   lose blood 피를 흘리다   operation 图 수술   ask A for B A에 B를 요청하다   supply 图 보급(품)
deliver 图 배달하다 (delivery 图 배달)   drone 图 드론(무인 항공기)   life-saving 图 생명을 살리는   land 图 착륙하다 图 육지
contain 图 ~이 들어 있다   medical 图 의료의   attach 图 붙이다   parachute 图 낙하산   perform 图 수행하다   save 图 살리다, 구하다; 절약하다
disaster 图 재해, 재난   reach 图 닿다, 도달하다   rescue 图 구조 图 구조하다   <문제> affect 图 영향을 주다   support 图 지원 图 지지하다
missing 图 실종된   medical care 건강 관리   emergency 图 응급 상황

Guy de Maupassant, a famous writer, used to have lunch every day at a restaurant inside the Eiffel Tower. He said, "It is the only place in Paris where I can sit and not actually see the tower!" Like him, many *Parisians hated the Eiffel Tower at first.

However, the tower was located in the city's center, so people naturally saw it every day. Over time, they got used to it and started to love it. This is an example of the familiarity principle. The more you are exposed to something, the more you like it.

You may have had this experience with advertisements. Advertisers use the same commercial repeatedly. At first, you may be indifferent or even annoyed by it. But later, you find yourself choosing the brand _____. Just like the Parisians and the Eiffel Tower, you get so familiar with it that you like it in the end.

*Parisian 파리 사람

Read & Learn

현대 단편소설의 아버지, 기 드 모파상(Guy de Maupassant)
프랑스의 소설가 모파상은 1880년에 발표한 첫 소설 「비곗덩어리」로 단번에 명성을 얻었고, 이후 10년 동안 약 300편의 단편소설을 썼어요. 그의 대표작으로는 「목걸이」, 「여자의 일생」이 있는데, 특히 「목걸이」는 주인공이 친구에게 빌린 목걸이를 잃어버린 사건을 다루며 지나친 욕심은 화를 부른다는 교훈을 전해주지요. 이렇듯 모파상은 파리 서민들의 일상을 관찰해 인생의 허무함, 고독함을 객관적이고 단조로운 문체로 그려냈어요.

1 모파상이 매일 에펠탑 안의 식당에서 점심을 먹은 이유는?

① 식당의 요리사가 매우 유명했기 때문에

② 에펠탑을 보지 않을 수 있었기 때문에

③ 파리 경치를 감상하며 식사할 수 있었기 때문에

④ 글을 쓰는 데 영감을 얻을 수 있었기 때문에

⑤ 에펠탑을 보러 온 사람들을 피할 수 있었기 때문에

● 서술형

2 시간이 지나면서 에펠탑에 대한 파리 사람들의 반응이 어떻게 달라졌는지 우리말로 쓰시오.

_____

3 이 글의 빈칸에 들어갈 말로 가장 적절한 것은?

① you have never heard of

② you trust the most

③ you have researched before

④ you saw in the commercial

⑤ your friends recommended

● 심화형

4 다음 중, 이 글에서 설명하는 원칙에 해당하는 사례를 말한 사람은?

① Woojin: It is hard to satisfy everyone.

② Nayoung: I try to give a good first impression to strangers.

③ Jihye: I want to follow what other people do.

④ Youngmin: As I meet my friends often, I become more fond of them.

⑤ Hyuna: If you change your point of view, familiar things can seem new.

Words

actually 倂사실상, 실제로 at first 처음에는 be located in ~에 위치해 있다 over time 시간이 지나면서 get used to ~에 익숙해지다
familiarity 圀친숙성, 친밀함 principle 圀원칙 be exposed to ~에 노출되다 experience 圀경험 圄경험하다
advertisement 圀광고 (advertiser 圀광고주) commercial 圀광고 圀상업적인 repeatedly 倂반복적으로 indifferent 圀무관심한
annoyed 圀짜증이 난 <문제> research 圄조사하다, 연구하다 recommend 圄추천하다 satisfy 圄만족시키다 impression 圀인상
fond of ~을 좋아하는 point of view 관점

If you've ever seen the Winter Olympics, you may have thought short-track skating and speed skating look very similar.   (A)   , these two are completely different sports. The most basic difference is the track length. The track for speed skating, which is 400 meters long, is around four times longer than that for short-track skating.

▲ 쇼트트랙 스케이팅

The rules are also quite different. In short-track skating, four to eight skaters compete at once. Because there are so many skaters on the track, passing competitors and navigating around them quickly are important skills. But in speed skating, only two skaters are on the ice, each skating in his or her own lane. Skaters only focus on going as fast as possible.

In addition, the blades of speed skates are long to provide more speed. The blades of short-track skates,   (B)   , are shorter so that the skaters can make turns more easily.

3

6

9

12

15

18

Read & Learn 종목별 스케이트화 날에 숨은 과학

· **쇼트트랙 스케이트화**: 날이 중심에서 왼쪽으로 치우쳐 있고 왼쪽으로 휘어 있어요. 선수들이 곡선 구간을 돌 때 속도 유지를 위해 몸을 최대한 왼쪽으로 기울이는 것에 맞춰 설계되었어요.
· **스피드 스케이트화**: 날의 뒤쪽이 분리되는 것이 특징이에요. 이는 곡선 구간을 돌 때에도 날은 빙판에 닿아있도록 해서 선수들이 빠른 속도로 나아갈 수 있어요.
· **피겨 스케이트화**: 날의 가운데에 홈이 파여 있고 앞쪽은 톱니 모양으로 만들어져 있어요. 오목한 홈은 빠른 방향 전환을, 톱니는 스핀과 점프를 할 수 있게 해준답니다.

1 이 글의 주제를 다음과 같이 나타낼 때, 빈칸에 들어갈 말을 글에서 찾아 쓰시오.

> two sports that look _____ but are actually _____

2 다음 질문에 대한 답이 되도록 빈칸에 들어갈 말을 우리말로 쓰시오.

> Q. What are significant abilities in short-track skating but not in speed skating?

A. 한 번에 최대 _____ 명까지의 선수들이 경기를 하기 때문에, 쇼트트랙 선수들은 _____ 기술과 그들 주위에서 빠르게 길을 찾는 기술을 갖춰야 한다.

3 이 글의 빈칸 (A)와 (B)에 들어갈 말로 가장 적절한 것은?

(A)		(B)
① Furthermore	......	therefore
② Therefore	......	however
③ Therefore	......	on the other hand
④ However	......	therefore
⑤ However	......	on the other hand

4 이 글의 내용으로 보아, 괄호 안에서 알맞은 말을 골라 표시하시오.

Length of Track	Short-track skating has a (1) (shorter / longer) track than speed skating.
Number of Skaters	Speed skating has (2) (fewer / more) skaters in one race than short-track skating.
Design of the Skates	Speed skating has (3) (shorter / longer) skate blades than short-track skating.

Words

similar 혱비슷한 completely 뮈완전히 basic 혱기본적인 difference 몡차이(점) track 몡트랙; 길 length 몡길이
compete 통겨루다, 경쟁하다 (competitor 몡경쟁자) at once 한 번에 pass 통추월하다, 통과하다 navigate 통길을 찾다
lane 몡레인, 경주로 blade 몡날 provide 통제공하다 make a turn 방향을 틀다 <문제> significant 혱중요한 ability 몡능력
furthermore 뮈게다가 on the other hand 반면에

People have started a new online challenge with a plastic bottle. It starts with closing the cap loosely. Then they kick the cap with the tips of their toes to open it. They record this and upload the video to their social media accounts. After that, the challenge is complete!

Actually, martial artists used to do this to increase the accuracy of their kicks. It became popular when some celebrities started doing it on social media, calling it the Bottle Cap Challenge.

Online challenges like this are just for fun. But many challenges are also carried out in the public interest. (A) As a result, lots of people learned about the disease. (B) The most famous one is the Ice Bucket Challenge, where people poured ice water over themselves. (C) It was started to raise awareness of *Lou Gehrig's disease, and tens of millions of people around the world participated.

*Lou Gehrig's disease 루게릭병 (근육을 통제하는 신경세포가 손상되는 병)

●심화형

1 What is the best title for the passage?

① How to Start Online Challenges

② Challenges for Fun and Public Good

③ Why People Like to Test Their Limits

④ Martial Arts That Became Challenges

⑤ Challenges: A New Way to Raise Funds

2 Write T if the statement about the Bottle Cap Challenge is true or F if it is false.

(1) It was started to increase awareness of martial arts. _____

(2) Celebrities started it on social media and named it. _____

3 What is the best order for sentences (A)~(C)?

① (A) – (B) – (C)   ② (B) – (A) – (C)   ③ (B) – (C) – (A)

④ (C) – (A) – (B)   ⑤ (C) – (B) – (A)

4 Choose the correct one based on the passage.

Bottle Cap Challenge Ⓐ   Ⓒ   Ice Bucket Challenge Ⓑ

Ⓐ: People originally did it to improve their (kicks / videos).

Ⓑ: It was intended to let people (understand / overcome) the disease.

Ⓒ: Both became famous online and attracted a lot of (patients / participants).

Words

challenge 명챌린지, 도전 동도전하다 cap 명뚜껑 loosely 분느슨하게 tip 명끝 record 동녹화하다 upload 동업로드하다
social media 소셜 미디어 account 명계정; 설명, 이야기 complete 형완료된; 완벽한 martial artist 무술가 accuracy 명정확성
celebrity 명유명인 carry out 실시하다, 수행하다 public interest 공익 disease 명병 bucket 명버킷, 양동이 pour 동붓다
awareness 명인식, 의식 participate 동참여하다 <문제> public good 공익 understand 동알다, 이해하다 overcome 동극복하다
attract 동마음을 끌다

1 다음 밑줄 친 단어와 가장 비슷한 의미의 단어는?

> Firefighters <u>saved</u> all of the people that were trapped in the building.

① rescued   ② tested   ③ affected   ④ researched   ⑤ supported

2 다음 밑줄 친 단어와 가장 반대되는 의미의 단어는?

> I used a hammer and nails to <u>attach</u> the shelf to the wall.

① navigate   ② upload   ③ deliver   ④ attract   ⑤ separate

[3-5] 다음 괄호 안에서 알맞은 단어를 골라 표시하시오.

3 This campaign raises public (ability / awareness) of environmental problems.

4 Our airplane will (land / lend) in Sydney in two hours.

5 Providing help at the charity event was a valuable (experience / difference).

[6-8] 다음 빈칸에 들어갈 단어나 표현을 보기에서 골라 쓰시오.

보기	carry out provide make a turn familiarity accident

6 Dane looked like my brother, so I felt a sense of _____.

7 The researchers will _____ an experiment to find the cause of climate change.

8 To keep the audience's attention, it is important to _____ interesting information.

[9-10] 다음 밑줄 친 단어나 표현에 유의하여 각 문장의 해석을 쓰시오.

9 The hospital <u>asks</u> the supply center <u>for</u> more blood.

→ _____

10 Over time, they <u>got used to</u> it and started to love it.

→ _____

환경보호에 참여하는 쿨~한 방법

트래시태그 챌린지 *challenge*

SNS상에서 자신의 개성을 마음껏 뽐낼 수 있는 챌린지, 다들 참여해봤어? 열심히 찍은 사진이나 영상에 '좋아요'를 많이 받으면 사실 시험에서 100점 맞은 것보다도 뿌듯하단 말이지! 여기 특별한 챌린지를 소개할게. 바로 트래시태그 #trashtag 챌린지야!

luv_727
남산공원 Namsan Park

Liked by mr_p2ce and 98 others
luv_727 #trashtag #trashtagchallenge

Q. 어떻게 시작됐어?

A. 트래시태그 챌린지는 미국의 한 야외 활동 전문가의 아이디어로부터 시작됐어. 그는 등산 중 산에 널려있는 쓰레기에 충격을 받고는 사람들이 스스로 쓰레기를 치우게 할 방법으로 이 챌린지를 아웃도어 의류 회사에 제안했다고 해. 처음부터 빵! 뜬 핫한 챌린지는 아니지만, **지구를 지속가능한 곳으로 만들자는** 목소리가 커지면서 **점점 더 많은 사람들이 이 챌린지에 참여**하는 중!

Q. 챌린지의 파급력이 대단하구나. 그런데 쓰레기 문제가 그렇게 심각해?

A. 우리나라에서 하루에 발생하는 쓰레기는 약 43만 톤이 넘는다고 해. 더 심각한 것은 매년 최고 기록이 경신되고 있다는 사실이지. 특히 강가나 산, 해변에 버려진 쓰레기들은 야생동물들에게 치명적이고 자연경관도 해치는 만큼 우리나라에서도 트래시태그 챌린지에 대한 활발한 참여가 필요해.

Q. 오, 뭔가 솔깃한데? 어떻게 참여해?

A. 참여 방법은 정말 간단해. 누구나 어디에서든 쓰레기를 치우고 그 인증샷을 SNS에 올리면 되거든. 그리고 인증샷에 #trashtag 태그를 붙이면 끝! SNS에서 태그를 검색해서 전 세계 곳곳에서 올라오는 인증샷을 구경하는 재미도 쏠쏠하다고. 쓰레기를 치우기 전과 후를 비교한 인증샷을 보면 내 속이 다 시원할 정도라니까! 어때, 우리도 한번 해보지 않을래?

HackersBook.com

UNIT 02

Have you ever tried Shooting Star ice cream? When you eat it, you can feel tiny explosions in your mouth. This is caused by candies called Pop Rocks. They provide a unique ³ sensation by popping as ⓐ they melt in your mouth. So what makes Pop Rocks pop?

The key is *carbon dioxide trapped inside the candy. To ⁶ make Pop Rocks, carbon dioxide gas is poured into sugar water. Then the mixture is frozen and broken into pieces. When you eat them, the outer layer of sugar melts and the ⁹ carbon dioxide gas escapes into the air. This causes the popping sensation in your mouth, as well as the cracking sound that comes with ⓑ it. ¹²

Carbon dioxide is also contained in many soft drinks. That's why it feels like bubbles are popping in your mouth when you drink ⓒ them! ¹⁵

*carbon dioxide 이산화탄소

Read & Learn 💥 **'빵' 터지는 조합**

파핑 캔디는 '탁'하고 터지는 느낌만 주지만, 이 두 음식은 같이 먹으면 정말 '빵'하고 터질 수도 있어요! 바로 콜라와 아이스크림이에요. 아이스크림은 재료를 섞고 얼리는 과정에서 공기와 닿게 되는데, 이때 생긴 기체 분자들이 콜라 속 이산화탄소와 만나면 빠르게 팽창해요. 따라서 콜라와 아이스크림을 함께 먹으면 기체가 몸속에서 빠른 속도로 팽창하게 되고, 구토를 유발해요. 심할 경우 급성 위확장 증세가 발생할 수 있으니 주의해야 해요!

1 이 글의 주제로 가장 적절한 것은?

① the role of sugar in food

② how to make frozen carbon dioxide

③ the dangers of carbon dioxide in food

④ how Pop Rocks cause an unusual sensation

⑤ different kinds of food containing Pop Rocks

2 이 글의 밑줄 친 the mixture를 구성하는 것을 우리말로 쓰시오.

_____

3 이 글의 밑줄 친 ⓐ, ⓑ, ⓒ가 가리키는 것을 글에서 찾아 쓰시오.

ⓐ: _____

ⓑ: _____

ⓒ: _____

4 이 글의 내용으로 보아, 다음 빈칸에 들어갈 말을 글에서 찾아 쓰시오.

> When you eat Pop Rocks, the frozen sugar layer _____ in your mouth. Then, the inner carbon dioxide gas _____ and gives you a popping sensation.

Words

tiny 휑작은 explosion 폥폭발 pop 통터지다 unique 휑독특한, 특별한 sensation 폥느낌, 감각 trap 통가두다 mixture 폥혼합물
freeze 통냉동시키다, 얼리다 (freeze-froze-frozen) break into pieces 여러 조각들로 부수다, 부서지다
outer 휑바깥의 (inner 휑안쪽의, 내부의) layer 폥층 melt 통녹다, 녹이다 escape 통빠져나오다, 도망가다 crack 통탁하고 깨지다, 금이 가다
come with ~과 함께 따라오다, ~이 딸려 있다 soft drink 탄산음료 bubble 폥방울

People often make reservations in advance for products or services. However, some customers never show up and don't cancel beforehand. These customers are called ₃ no-shows.

No-shows _____. For example, some people may not be able to board a train or plane ₆ because of unused tickets bought by no-shows. In the restaurant business, no-shows are even worse. They can damage the business itself. (a) Customers sometimes make ₉ reservations or order food in advance. (b) Good service at the restaurant is as important to customers as the food. (c) If the people don't come, the restaurant doesn't get paid ₁₂ for the work and the food goes to waste. (d) In addition, the restaurant loses an opportunity to accept other customers while waiting for the no-show. (e) The loss is even bigger ₁₅ when the no-show is a large group.

Nowadays, many businesses try to prevent no-shows by charging ahead of time or making a blacklist. But no-shows ₁₈ still remain a problem for businesses.

1 이 글의 제목으로 가장 적절한 것은?

① Why Do No-shows Happen A Lot?

② An Effective Way to Prevent No-shows

③ The Future of the Restaurant Businesses

④ Customers Who Can Damage Businesses

⑤ Efforts of Businesses to Satisfy Customers

2 이 글의 빈칸에 들어갈 말로 가장 적절한 것은?

① buy lots of products at once

② usually don't make reservations

③ want to reschedule their appointments

④ ask for more services from businesses

⑤ cause problems for other customers

3 이 글의 (a)~(e) 중, 전체 흐름과 관계<u>없는</u> 문장은?

① (a)　　　② (b)　　　③ (c)　　　④ (d)　　　⑤ (e)

(서술형)

4 사업체들이 no-shows를 막기 위해 하는 일 두 가지를 우리말로 쓰시오.

(1) _____

(2) _____

(Words)

make a reservation 예약을 하다　in advance 미리　product 圐제품　customer 圐고객, 손님　show up 나타나다　cancel 통취소하다
beforehand 閳사전에　board 통탑승하다 圐판자　damage 통피해를 입히다　order 통주문하다; 명령하다　go to waste 낭비되다
lose 통잃다, 분실하다 (loss 圐손해, 손실)　opportunity 圐기회　accept 통받다, 받아들이다　prevent 통막다　charge 통요금을 청구하다
ahead of time 미리　blacklist 圐블랙리스트(특별히 주의하고 감시할 필요가 있는 인물의 명단)　<문제> effective 圐효과적인
satisfy 통만족시키다　at once 한꺼번에; 즉시　reschedule 통일정을 변경하다　appointment 圐예약, 약속

Getting a gift for a boyfriend or girlfriend can be (A) easy / difficult. This is especially true when he or she is from another country. Here are a few examples of why it's important to understand a culture when you give gifts.

In Vietnam, cups and handkerchiefs are very (B) good / bad gifts. For Vietnamese people, cups symbolize the end of a relationship since they often crack or break. _____, handkerchiefs are not appropriate because they are used to dry a person's tears. In other words, they represent sadness after a breakup.

Meanwhile, in Russia, flowers are a favorite gift, but you must be careful when giving them. Never give yellow flowers as they are thought to be bad luck. In addition, always give bouquets with an (C) odd / even number of flowers. Even numbers of flowers are only given at funerals.

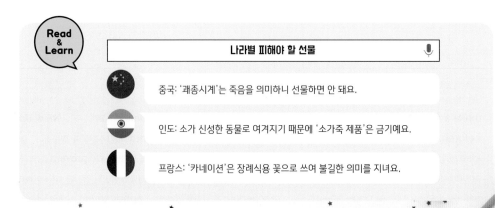

나라별 피해야 할 선물

중국: '괘종시계'는 죽음을 의미하니 선물하면 안 돼요.

인도: 소가 신성한 동물로 여겨지기 때문에 '소가죽 제품'은 금기예요.

프랑스: '카네이션'은 장례식용 꽃으로 쓰여 불길한 의미를 지녀요.

1 (A), (B), (C)의 각 네모 안에서 문맥에 알맞은 말로 가장 적절한 것은?

	(A)		(B)		(C)
①	easy	……	bad	……	even
②	easy	……	good	……	even
③	difficult	……	bad	……	even
④	difficult	……	good	……	odd
⑤	difficult	……	bad	……	odd

2 이 글의 빈칸에 들어갈 말로 가장 적절한 것은?

① Instead   ② Similarly   ③ Otherwise

④ On the other hand   ⑤ For example

3 이 글의 내용과 일치하도록 다음 빈칸에 들어갈 말을 글에서 찾아 쓰시오.

In Vietnam	Cups are symbols of the (1) _____ _____ _____ _____ .
In Russia	Yellow flowers are considered (2) _____ _____ .

• 서술형

4 이 글의 밑줄 친 부분의 이유를 유추하여 우리말로 쓰시오.

_____

Words

especially 뷛특히 **Vietnam** 몡베트남 (**Vietnamese** 혱베트남의) **handkerchief** 몡손수건 **symbolize** 됭상징하다 **relationship** 몡관계 **crack** 됭금이 가다 **appropriate** 혱적절한 **dry one's tears** ~의 눈물을 닦다 **represent** 됭나타내다; 대표하다 **breakup** 몡이별 **meanwhile** 뷛한편 **bouquet** 몡꽃다발 **odd** 혱홀수의; 이상한 **even** 혱짝수의; 평평한 **funeral** 몡장례식 <문제> **similarly** 뷛비슷하게 **otherwise** 뷛그렇지 않으면 **consider** 됭여기다, 고려하다

How long do you think it takes to build a house?

(A) Surprisingly, a single 3D-printed house takes only about a day to build. (B) With this program, it can be built by a small crew of four to six people in a day. (C) It doesn't even require a lot of workers to construct it because the 3D printer is controlled by special software on a tablet. The workers just have to watch the printer building the basic structure and make a few adjustments. This structure is so _____ that the house can withstand extreme weather. It can even remain standing through hurricanes and earthquakes. Best of all, it costs only about $10,000 to build a brand-new home!

As technology improves, 3D-printed houses will become cheaper and faster to build, and their quality will increase. In the future, we may be able to make entire cities with the push of a button.

▲ 3D 프린터로 집을 짓는 과정　　▲ 3D 프린터로 지은 집

1 What is the best order for sentences (A)~(C)?

① (A) – (B) – (C)　　② (A) – (C) – (B)　　③ (B) – (A) – (C)

④ (B) – (C) – (A)　　⑤ (C) – (A) – (B)

심화형

2 Which is the best choice to complete the sentence?

> A 3D-printed house doesn't need many workers to build it because ＿＿＿＿＿＿＿.

① the 3D printer works at high speed

② the workers only construct the basic structure

③ the 3D printer doesn't require any adjustments

④ the workers only have to oversee the printer's work

⑤ only a few skilled workers can control the 3D printer

3 Which is the best choice for the blank?

① small　　　　② strong　　　　③ clean

④ economical　　⑤ comfortable

4 Complete the table about 3D-printed houses. Write the answers in Korean.

Construction Period	약 (1) ＿＿＿＿＿＿
Strength	폭풍과 (2) ＿＿＿＿＿＿까지 견딜 수 있다.
Cost	약 (3) ＿＿＿＿＿
Expectations	더 저렴하고 빠르게 지을 수 있을 것이고, (4) ＿＿＿＿＿ 것이다.

Words

3D-printed 혱 3D 프린터로 만든　**crew** 몡 무리　**require** 통 필요로 하다　**construct** 통 건설하다 (**construction** 몡 건설, 공사)
software 몡 소프트웨어　**tablet** 몡 태블릿; 알약　**structure** 몡 구조(물)　**adjustment** 몡 조정　**withstand** 통 견디다　**extreme** 혱 극심한
hurricane 몡 폭풍　**earthquake** 몡 지진　**brand-new** 혱 완전히 새로운, 신제품의　**technology** 몡 기술　**improve** 통 개선되다, 향상시키다
quality 몡 품질　**entire** 혱 전체의　<문제> **oversee** 통 감독하다　**skilled** 혱 숙련된　**economical** 혱 경제적인, 알뜰한　**strength** 몡 장점; 힘
expectations 몡 기대되는 점; (단수형) 예상

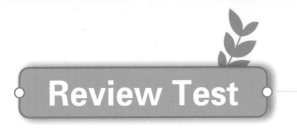
[1-3] 단어와 영영 풀이를 알맞게 연결하시오.

1 expectation •   • ⓐ the ability to feel something physically

2 appropriate •   • ⓑ the belief or feeling that something will happen in the future

3 sensation •   • ⓒ right for a particular situation or purpose

4 다음 밑줄 친 단어와 가장 비슷한 의미의 단어는?

> The game <u>satisfied</u> customers who had to wait in line to buy it.

① prevented   ② pleased   ③ surprised   ④ remembered   ⑤ annoyed

[5-8] 다음 빈칸에 들어갈 단어를 [보기]에서 골라 쓰시오.

보기	construction appointment oversee board explosion

5 The team worked hard on the _____ of the hotel to build it as quickly as possible.

6 Every passenger must _____ the ship before it leaves.

7 The manager of the restaurant has to _____ the kitchen workers and the waiters.

8 Emma had an _____ with the dentist this afternoon, but she forgot about it.

[9-10] 다음 밑줄 친 단어나 표현에 유의하여 각 문장의 해석을 쓰시오.

9 Then the mixture is frozen and <u>broken into pieces</u>.

→ _____

10 People often <u>make reservations</u> in advance for products or services.

→ _____

로망을 현실로 만드는 셀프 인테리어

감성 충만
방 꾸미기

나만의 스타일로 꾸며진 쾌적하고 아늑한 방!
누구나 꿈꾸는 로망이죠?
내 취향대로 방을 바꿀 수 있는 쉬운
셀프 인테리어 비법을 전수할게요!

반려 식물로 싱그러운 분위기 UP!

작은 화분을 방에 들여놓는 것만으로도 방 분위기를 생기 있게 만들 수 있어요. 식물을
키우기만 하면 시들시들해져 키우는 게 부담스럽다고요? 걱정할 필요 없어요. 선인장,
다육식물 등 키우기 쉬운 식물도 참 많답니다. 다양한 종류의 식물들을 들여놓으면 방 안
분위기가 금세 감성적인 카페처럼 변신할 거예요.

포스터를 이용해 개성 넘치는
방 만들기

심심한 벽을 감각적으로 꾸미는 가장 쉬운 방법은
바로 포스터 붙이기예요. 연예인, 영화, 야구, 만화 등
무엇이든 좋아요. 평소 관심 있는 분야의 포스터를
적극적으로 활용해서 개성을 표현해보세요. 벽에
걸 수 있는 패브릭 포스터를 이용하거나, 네트 망에
사진이나 인형을 달아 직접 벽 한쪽을 꾸며도
포인트가 된답니다.

포스터 붙이는 꿀팁

1. **네일팁 양면테이프**: 작지만, 접착력이 강해 테이프가 잘 붙지 않는 오돌토돌한 벽지에도 착 달라붙어요.
2. **마스킹 테이프 + 클립 + 자석**: 벽에 마스킹 테이프로 클립을 붙여요. 그 위에 포스터를 올리고 자석으로 고정하면 끝!
3. **자석 테이프**: 포스터 모서리 부분에 붙여 사용해요. 대신, 자석이라서 건들면 떨어질 수도 있어요.
4. **코너 스티커**: 모서리 부분에 붙이는 코너 스티커를 이용하면 소중한 내 최애 포스터를 보호할 수 있어요.

HackersBook.com

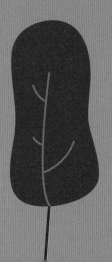

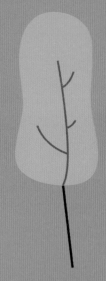

UNIT 03

▲ 지문 음성 바로 듣기

You can get 24 Christmas gifts with this special calendar! It's called an *Advent calendar. It has 24 little "doors," and there is a different gift behind each one. From December 1, you open one door a day. You _____ every day until Christmas.

Usually, Advent calendars contain chocolates, sweets, or Christmas decorations. (①) Sometimes, <u>more special items</u> are found inside them. (②) Beauty product samples or popular character figures can be behind the doors! (③) You can fill it with letters or photos and give it to your family or friends. (④) You can include whatever the receiver likes, so the handmade calendars are more personal. (⑤)

Advent calendars let you enjoy every day you spend waiting for Christmas. What sort of presents would you like to get from the calendar?

*Advent 강림절 (기독교에서 크리스마스 전 4주간을 가리키는 말)

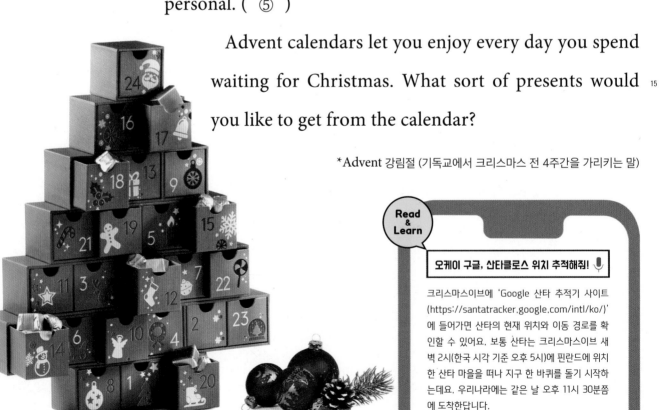

Read & Learn

오케이 구글, 산타클로스 위치 추적해줘! 🎤

크리스마스이브에 'Google 산타 추적기 사이트 (https://santatracker.google.com/intl/ko/)' 에 들어가면 산타의 현재 위치와 이동 경로를 확인할 수 있어요. 보통 산타는 크리스마스이브 새벽 2시(한국 시각 기준 오후 5시)에 핀란드에 위치한 산타 마을을 떠나 지구 한 바퀴를 돌기 시작하는데요. 우리나라에는 같은 날 오후 11시 30분쯤에 도착한답니다.

• • •

https://santatracker.google.com/intl/ko/

1 이 글의 빈칸에 들어갈 말로 가장 적절한 것은?

① write a card ② make a wish

③ decorate a house ④ mark on a calendar

⑤ receive a surprise

2 이 글의 흐름으로 보아, 다음 문장이 들어가기에 가장 적절한 곳은?

> You can also make your own Advent calendar.

① ② ③ ④ ⑤

3 이 글의 밑줄 친 more special items에 해당하는 것을 우리말로 쓰시오.

_____

4 이 글에서 강림절 달력에 관해 언급되지 <u>않은</u> 것은?

① 달력에 넣는 선물의 개수 ② 달력을 사용하는 시기

③ 달력을 구매하는 방법 ④ 달력에 넣는 선물의 종류

⑤ 수제 달력의 특징

Words

calendar 몡 달력 **sweets** 몡 사탕; (단수형) 단맛 **decoration** 몡 장식 (**decorate** 동 꾸미다, 장식하다) **sample** 몡 샘플, 표본
figure 몡 인형, 피겨 **fill** 동 채우다 **include** 동 넣다, 포함하다 **receiver** 몡 받는 사람 (**receive** 동 받다) **handmade** 형 수제의
personal 형 개인적인 **sort** 몡 종류 <문제> **make a wish** 소원을 빌다 **mark** 동 표시하다

Many types of bacteria live in your mouth. Among them, there are harmful bacteria that cause tooth decay. *S. mutans, for example, is actually the main cause of tooth decay. This type of bacteria usually gets energy from ⓐ the sugar in the food you eat. However, there is ⓑ something sweet that S. mutans can't digest. It's a natural sweetener called **xylitol. ⓒ It has chemical qualities similar to those of sugar. For this reason, when you eat xylitol, the S. mutans bacteria mistake ⓓ it for sugar and consume it. But they cannot digest xylitol, so they get no energy from ⓔ it. After a few attempts to eat xylitol, the bacteria finally run out of energy, die, and fall out of your mouth. In other words, xylitol causes them to starve to death!

*S. mutans 뮤탄스균 (주된 충치 유발균)　**xylitol 자일리톨

OX 퀴즈! 자일리톨을 섭취하면 충치가 잘 안 생긴다?
정답은 O! 자일리톨 껌을 씹는 것을 통해서도 쉽게 자일리톨을 섭취할 수 있는데, 특히 자기 전에 씹는 것이 충치 예방에 더 효과적이라고 해요. 또한, 입안에 음식물이 남아 있는 상태에서 자일리톨을 섭취하면 효과가 떨어진다고 하니, 자일리톨을 섭취하기 전 양치는 꼭 하는 것이 좋아요. 알겠죠? 휘바, 휘바!
*단, 설탕과 같은 성분이 들어 있는 껌을 고르지 않도록 주의하세요!

1 이 글의 제목으로 가장 적절한 것은?

① Harmful Bacteria in Some Food

② The Effect of Xylitol on Bacteria

③ Surprising Causes of Tooth Decay

④ How Xylitol Provides Our Body with Energy

⑤ You Should Avoid Sugar to Protect Your Teeth

2 이 글의 밑줄 친 ⓐ~ⓔ 중, 가리키는 대상이 나머지 넷과 <u>다른</u> 것은?

① ⓐ   ② ⓑ   ③ ⓒ   ④ ⓓ   ⑤ ⓔ

3 이 글의 내용과 일치하지 <u>않는</u> 것은?

① 입안에는 다양한 종류의 세균이 있다.

② 뮤탄스균은 충치의 주원인이다.

③ 자일리톨은 설탕과 비슷한 화학적 성질을 가지고 있다.

④ 입안의 세균은 자일리톨을 피해 도망간다.

⑤ 자일리톨은 뮤탄스균을 죽게 만든다.

4 이 글의 내용으로 보아, 다음 빈칸에 들어갈 말을 글에서 찾아 쓰시오.

> S. Mutans is one type of _____ bacteria in your mouth. It confuses xylitol with _____ and eats xylitol. However, it starves to death because it can't _____ xylitol.

Words

bacteria 몡세균, 박테리아 (단수형: bacterium) harmful 휑해로운 tooth decay 충치 digest 통소화하다 natural 휑천연의, 자연의 sweetener 몡감미료 chemical 휑화학적인 quality 몡성질; 품질 mistake A for B A를 B로 착각하다 consume 통먹다; 소비하다 attempt 몡시도 run out of ~을 다 써버리다 fall out of ~에서 떨어져 나오다 starve to death 굶어 죽다

<문제> provide A with B A에게 B를 제공하다 confuse A with B A와 B를 혼동하다

Imagine a woman looking through a basket of peaches at a grocery store. After selecting one of the fruits, she doesn't go to a checkout counter to pay. Instead, she scans a QR code with her phone, and the payment is made! 3

In China, this is a common method for buying things. Apps such as AliPay and WeChat Pay are connected to users' bank accounts, and their payments are automatically transferred when they scan the QR codes. This not only makes it unnecessary to 6 9 12

carry around cash or credit cards but also makes processing payments much faster and simpler.

Now, the technology is so popular that it can be seen all across the country. Even street performers and musicians accept tips this way. Many believe it will soon become the main form of payment in other parts of the world, too. 15 18

SCAN

Read & Learn

알아두면 유용한 상식! QR 코드 이야기

Quick Response code, 즉 QR 코드는 글자 그대로 풀이하면 '빠르게 응답하는 코드'라는 뜻이에요. 90년대에 일본의 한 제조회사가 제품 정보를 편리하게 기록하기 위해 QR 코드를 개발해 사용하기 시작했는데요. 이전까지는 12~13개의 글자나 숫자만 기록할 수 있는 막대기 모양의 바코드를 사용했어요. 이 때문에 날이 갈수록 다양해지는 제품들을 모두 기록하기에는 어려움이 많았다고 해요. 이와 달리 QR 코드는 글자는 4,296자까지, 숫자는 무려 7,089개까지 기록할 수 있답니다.

1 이 글의 제목으로 가장 적절한 것은?

① How Do Phones Read QR Codes?

② QR Codes: A Convenient Way to Pay

③ What is the Best Banking App in China?

④ Useful Information Stored in QR Codes

⑤ New Technology Can Help Save Money

• 서술형

2 QR 코드를 이용한 결제 방식의 장점 두 가지를 우리말로 쓰시오.

(1) _____

(2) _____

3 이 글의 내용과 일치하면 T, 그렇지 않으면 F를 쓰시오.

(1) By using AliPay or WeChat Pay, people don't have to pay at the checkout counter.

_____

(2) Giving a tip to street performers via QR codes is not permitted in China yet.

_____

4 이 글의 내용으로 보아, 다음 빈칸에 들어갈 말을 보기 에서 골라 쓰시오.

보기	automatically	accept	pay	unnecessarily

In China, people can scan a QR code to _____ for things. Because money is _____ sent to the store, this convenient technology is now used nationwide.

Words

look through ~을 살펴보다, 훑어보다   **grocery** 몡식료품   **store** 몡상점 통저장하다   **select** 통고르다   **checkout counter** 계산대
scan 통스캔하다; 살피다   **payment** 몡결제 (금액)   **method** 몡방식, 방법   **connect** 통연결하다   **bank account** 은행 계좌
automatically 몪자동으로   **transfer** 통옮기다   **unnecessary** 혱불필요한 (**unnecessarily** 몪불필요하게)   **carry around** 가지고 다니다
credit card 신용카드   **tip** 몡팁, 사례금; 조언   <문제> **convenient** 혱편리한   **permit** 통허용하다, 허락하다   **nationwide** 몪전국적으로

Have you ever noticed the stitches on a baseball? Most baseballs have exactly 108 red double stitches on their surface. Interestingly, these stitches aren't just for show. Without them, the game of baseball wouldn't be the same as it is now.

Generally, smooth surfaces have less air resistance. (①) However, fast flying balls are different. (②) When a ball without stitches travels in the air, the opposing *airflow moves along the surface of the ball. (③) This pulls the ball backward and makes it fly slower. (④) But the stitches interrupt the airflow, which causes the air to change directions and bounce off the ball. (⑤)

This design also allows players to throw various types of pitches, including fast balls, curve balls, and others. Therefore, the little red stitches are quite important in baseball!

*airflow 기류

Read & Learn

포심 패스트볼과 투심 패스트볼

 가장 빠른 공, 포심(four-seam)
공을 쥘 때, 손가락이 공의 실밥(seam)에 닿는 부분이 4곳이면 포심이라고 해요. 이 방법으로 공을 던지면 공이 직선으로 빠르게 날아가는데, 대부분의 투수들이 이렇게 공을 쥔다고 해요.

 빠르면서도 강력한 공, 투심(two-seam)
투심은 손가락이 실밥에 닿는 부분이 2곳이에요. 투심으로 쥐는 공은 포심공과 비슷한 속도로 직선으로 날아가다가 좌우로 휘어져요. 따라서 공의 방향을 예측하기가 어려워서 헛스윙이 나오기 쉽답니다.

1 What is the best title for the passage?

① Smaller Ball, Faster Speed

② Important Roles of Baseball Stitches

③ How to Throw a Baseball More Accurately

④ The Long History of Professional Baseball

⑤ Red Stitches: A Great Design from a Small Mistake

 심화형

2 Where is the best place for the sentence?

> So, the air can't drag the ball back.

①   ②   ③   ④   ⑤

3 Complete the table with words from the passage.

The Movement of the Air When a Baseball Flies Fast

Baseballs (1) _____ Stitches	Baseballs with Stitches
The air will pull the ball back and make it move (2) _____.	The air will (3) _____ off the ball, so the ball will have less (4) _____ _____.

4 Which CANNOT be answered based on the passage?

① How many stitches are on a baseball?

② What does airflow do to flying balls?

③ How fast can a baseball fly through the air?

④ How do the stitches on a baseball affect airflow?

⑤ What lets players throw different pitches?

Words

notice 图알아차리다 stitch 图실밥, 바늘땀 surface 图표면 generally 图일반적으로 smooth 图매끄러운 resistance 图저항(력) travel 图이동하다; 여행하다 opposing 图반대의 pull 图잡아당기다 backward 图뒤로 interrupt 图방해하다 direction 图방향 bounce 图튕기다, 튀다 pitch 图투구 fast ball 속구 curve ball 커브볼 quite 图꽤 <문제> accurately 图정확하게 professional 图프로의, 전문적인 drag 图끌어당기다 movement 图움직임

1 다음 빈칸에 공통으로 들어갈 단어로 가장 적절한 것은?

- We should _____ enough protein to build muscles.
- This homework is going to _____ a lot of time to finish.

① digest   ② spend   ③ consume   ④ bake   ⑤ fill

2 다음 밑줄 친 단어와 가장 반대되는 의미의 단어는?

This product causes harmful effects on the skin, so we should avoid using it.

① personal   ② convenient   ③ various   ④ safe   ⑤ graceful

[3-5] 다음 영영 풀이에 해당하는 단어를 보기 에서 골라 뜻과 함께 쓰시오.

보기	decoration	interrupt	surface	method	bounce

		단어	뜻
3	a way of doing something	_____	_____
4	to stop someone or something for a short period	_____	_____
5	the outside or top layer of something	_____	_____

[6-8] 다음 빈칸에 들어갈 단어나 표현을 보기 에서 골라 쓰시오.

보기	run out of	attempt	carry around	transfer	permit

6 My phone will soon _____ energy if I don't charge it now.

7 I often _____ money to others using my smartphone.

8 On his first _____, the athlete broke the previous record.

[9-10] 다음 밑줄 친 단어나 표현에 유의하여 각 문장의 해석을 쓰시오.

9 In other words, xylitol causes them to starve to death!

→ _____

10 Imagine a woman looking through a basket of peaches at a grocery store.

→ _____

네 정체가 money?

우리 생활에서 떼려야 뗄 수 없는 존재, 돈!
가까이 있기에 오히려 잘 몰랐던 지폐에 대한 이야기를 함께
살펴볼까요?

지폐의 생로병사

우리나라 화폐는 한국은행의 주문을 받아 조폐공사에서 태어납니다. 금속으로
만든 동전은 조선 시대의 것이 그대로 발견될 만큼 그 생애가 아주 길지만, 종이
형태인 지폐의 수명은 그리 길지 않아요.

가장 수명이 짧은 지폐는 천 원권으로, 약 3년 4개월 동안 시중에 유통되다
수명을 다한답니다. 잔돈으로 사용되는 천 원권은 사람들의 손을 많이 타서
다른 종류의 지폐보다 수명이 짧은 편이거든요. 닳고 찢어져서 폐기되는 경우도
있지만, 화재, 낙서 등으로 훼손되어 쓸 수 없게 되는 경우도 많아요.

돈 냄새의 출처는?

"그 사람 돈 냄새는 기가 막히게 맡는군, 후후.." 느와르 영화에서 등장하는 단골
대사죠. 돈을 벌 방법이 뭔지를 알아챈다는 것을 '돈 냄새를 맡는다'라고 비유한
것인데, 실제로도 돈에서는 특유의 냄새가 나요. 이 특유의 냄새는 바로 잉크에서
비롯된 것이랍니다.

지폐는 여러 단계를 거쳐서 인쇄되는데, 이때 사용되는 특수 잉크들이 섞이고
건조되면서 특유의 향을 만들어내요. 이 향을 담은 향수도 출시되었다고 하니 '돈
냄새'를 풍기고 싶을 때 뿌리면 제격이겠네요!

지폐에는 왜 사람 얼굴이?

지폐는 모든 국민이 사용하는 데다가 외국에서도 거래되기 때문에 '나라의 얼굴'
이라고 할 정도로 상징성이 높아요. 따라서 일반적으로 그 나라를 대표할 수 있고
국민이 본받을 만한 위인의 얼굴이 들어가죠. 만 원권의 세종대왕처럼요!

또한, 지폐에 들어갈 그림으로 사람의 얼굴을 선호하는 데에는 위조 방지의
목적도 있어요. 사람의 얼굴은 다른 그림보다 디테일이 많고 섬세해 모방하기가
쉽지 않기 때문이에요.

HackersBook.com

UNIT 04

Czech people really love their *marionettes. These are a kind of puppet controlled by moving wires or strings. Marionette shows are common during Czech festivals, ₃ especially ones that celebrate the nation's independence. But what do these puppet shows have to do with independence?

In the 17th century, Czech lands were under **Habsburg ₆ rule. During that time, people were forced to use German, the language of their invaders. Conversations, documents, and even plays had to be in German. ___(A)___, the ₉ small puppet shows that were held in homes and alleys could still be performed in Czech. This helped people preserve their native language. They also built up hopes ₁₂ and dreams for independence through these puppet shows. Since the country gained its ___(B)___, the marionettes have become a significant part of the culture. ₁₅

*marionette 마리오네트, 꼭두각시 (인형)
**Habsburg 합스부르크 왕가 (13~20세기 사이의 옛 오스트리아 왕가)

1 이 글의 주제로 가장 적절한 것은?

① the world's oldest marionette

② the best way to enjoy Czech festivals

③ how to make puppets for marionette shows

④ why marionettes are important in Czech culture

⑤ the difference between Czech and German plays

2 이 글의 빈칸 (A)에 들어갈 말로 가장 적절한 것은?

① For instance　　　② Besides　　　③ However

④ In other words　　　⑤ Otherwise

(심화형)

3 이 글의 빈칸 (B)에 들어갈 말로 가장 적절한 것은?

① name　　　② wealth　　　③ support

④ freedom　　　⑤ popularity

4 이 글의 내용으로 보아, 다음 빈칸에 공통으로 들어갈 말을 글에서 찾아 쓰시오.

In the 17th century, Czech people had to use their invaders' _____, but they held marionette shows in their own _____.

Words

Czech 혱체코의 몡체코어　**puppet** 몡인형, 꼭두각시　**wires** 몡(꼭두각시를 조종하는) 실; (단수형) 철사; 전선　**string** 몡줄, 끈

celebrate 동축하하다　**independence** 몡독립　**have to do with** ~과 관련이 있다　**rule** 몡통치　**force** 동강요하다　**invader** 몡침략자

conversation 몡대화　**document** 몡문서　**play** 몡연극 동놀다　**alley** 몡골목　**preserve** 동보존하다　**native language** 모국어

build up ~을 키우다, 강화하다　**significant** 혱중요한　<문제> **wealth** 몡부　**freedom** 몡자유　**popularity** 몡인기

Can humans grow plants in space? It seems impossible because it's hard to provide plants with water, light, and gravity in space. Yet, astronauts have found ways to solve this problem!

▲ 국제 우주 정거장 내 Veggie의 모습

Veggie—also known as the Vegetable Production System—is a space garden on the *International Space Station. To grow plants on the Earth, we only need to place a seed or roots in dirt and regularly provide water. (①) Without gravity, the soil does not settle in pots around the plants. (②) So Veggie's plants are grown in a container of water. (③) Their roots are fixed with a special gum that helps the plants grow in one place. (④) Furthermore, LED lights installed above the plants guide the stems to grow upward. (⑤) In this way, gardening has become possible in space. Soon, we might be able to see a space farm with various plants!

*International Space Station 국제 우주 정거장

Read & Learn

궁금한 맛 이야기 Y

우주비행사들은 무엇을 먹고 살까?
우주에서는 음식이 쉽게 상하고 요리를 하는 것도 어렵기 때문에, 우주비행사는 특수 가공된 우주 식품을 먹어요.
우주 식품은 우주선의 무게를 줄이기 위해 동결 건조되거나 저온에서 급속 냉동한 후 물 분자를 빼내어 블록 형태로 만들어지는데, 생각보다 그 종류가 다양하다고 해요. 김치, 라면, 수정과, 비빔밥, 불고기와 같은 한식도 있답니다!

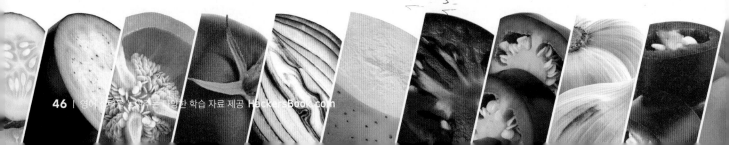

1 이 글의 제목을 다음과 같이 나타낼 때, 빈칸에 들어갈 말을 글에서 찾아 쓰시오.
(단, 주어진 철자로 시작하여 쓰시오.)

Growing P＿＿＿＿＿ in a S＿＿＿＿＿＿＿ Garden Called Veggie

• 서술형

2 이 글의 밑줄 친 this problem이 의미하는 내용을 우리말로 쓰시오.

＿＿＿＿＿＿＿＿＿＿＿＿＿＿＿＿＿＿＿＿＿＿＿＿＿＿＿＿＿

3 이 글의 흐름으로 보아, 다음 문장이 들어가기에 가장 적절한 곳은?

However, this doesn't work in space.

①　　　　　②　　　　　③　　　　　④　　　　　⑤

4 Veggie의 구성 요소와 각각의 역할을 알맞게 연결하시오.

(A) a water container　•　　　• (1) to prevent the roots from moving

(B) a special gum　　•　　　• (2) to replace the soil in zero gravity

(C) LED lights　　　•　　　• (3) to help the stems grow upward

5 이 글의 내용으로 보아, 다음 빈칸에 들어갈 말을 보기에서 골라 쓰시오.

보기　　gardening　natural　landing　farm　artificial

Recently, astronauts have invented a new ＿＿＿＿＿＿＿ method that uses water, gum, and ＿＿＿＿＿＿＿ lights to grow plants in the conditions of space. One day, we may even run a space ＿＿＿＿＿＿＿.

Words

provide A with B A에게 B를 제공하다　gravity 圆중력　astronaut 圆우주 비행사　production 圆생산　seed 圆씨앗　root 圆뿌리

dirt 圆흙　regularly 閉주기적으로　soil 圆흙　settle 图고정되다; (논쟁 등을) 해결하다　pot 圆화분　container 圆용기, 그릇

fix 图고정시키다; 수리하다　gum 圆고무　install 图설치하다　stem 圆줄기　upward 閉위로　gardening 圆원예

<문제> work 图잘되다, 유효하게 작용하다; 일하다　replace 图대체하다　artificial 圈인공의, 인공적인　conditions 圆환경; (단수형) 상태; 조건

run 图운영하다

The human eye is an incredible organ. Each one contains as many as 1.6 million nerve fibers. These fibers send signals to your brain, which processes what you see. However, there ₃ is a tiny spot in each eye that does not have any nerves. This is called the blind spot. You cannot see anything that comes in this area. But you normally do not realize it. Why? ₆ Your brain immediately fills in the image using information gathered from the other eye. Therefore, you think you have full vision, but part of it is actually created by your brain. ₉

You can check your blind spot with this test. Cover your right eye and stare at the green heart. Slowly move your face  closer, but keep focusing on it. At some point, you may ₁₅ suddenly notice that the red heart has disappeared. This happens when the red heart is in your _____.

1 첫 번째 단락의 내용을 다음과 같이 나타낼 때, 빈칸에 들어갈 말을 글에서 찾아 쓰시오.

> You see something with your eyes.

⌄

> Nerve fibers send (1) _____ to the (2) _____.

⌄

> The brain fills in the image with (3) _____ from the other eye.

⌄

> You perceive what the brain processes and creates.

2 이 글의 내용과 일치하면 T, 그렇지 않으면 F를 쓰시오.

(1) 양쪽 눈에는 약 320만 개의 신경 섬유가 있다. _____

(2) 맹점 안에 들어오는 사물은 볼 수 없으나, 우리는 보통 이를 인식하지 못한다. _____

3 이 글의 빈칸에 들어갈 말을 글에서 찾아 쓰시오.

_____ _____

4 이 글의 밑줄 친 this test의 과정과 일치하도록 괄호 안에서 알맞은 말을 골라 표시하시오.

(1) (왼쪽 / 오른쪽) 눈을 가리고, 초록색 하트를 응시한다.
(2) 초록색 하트에 초점을 둔 채 천천히 얼굴을 (가까이 / 멀리) 한다.
(3) 어느 시점에, (빨간색 / 초록색) 하트가 사라진다.

Words

incredible 혱 놀라운, 믿을 수 없는 organ 몡 기관, 장기 as many as 무려 ~개의, 무려 ~이나 되는 nerve 몡 신경 fiber 몡 섬유 signal 몡 신호
process 통 처리하다, 가공하다 몡 과정 blind spot 맹점 normally 閈 보통, 일반적으로 realize 통 알아차리다, 인식하다
immediately 閈 즉각적으로, 즉시 fill in ~을 채워 넣다, 채우다 gather 통 모으다, 모이다 vision 몡 시야, 시력 cover 통 가리다, 덮다
stare at ~을 응시하다 focus on ~에 초점을 맞추다, ~에 집중하다 disappear 통 사라지다 <문제> perceive 통 인식하다

"To be, or not to be, that is the question." This is the most famous line from the play *Hamlet*. (A) As a result, you might delay making choices or let others decide for you. (B) In the play, Hamlet, the main character, faces a situation where he struggles to make a decision. (C) Like him, you may have a hard time making decisions in some cases.

But if this happens frequently, you could have a condition known as Hamlet Syndrome. People with this syndrome are afraid they will make the wrong choice. Even an everyday decision like choosing what to drink can be stressful. To these people, having many options means that _____!

Interestingly, some restaurants see this phenomenon as an opportunity to attract more customers. They provide a special menu each day with a single item for people who can't make a choice. They even have a menu item for so-called Hamlets: *Whatever*.

Read & Learn

또 다른 현대인의 질환, FOMO 증후군

최근 햄릿 증후군뿐만 아니라 FOMO 증후군을 겪는 사람들도 많다고 해요. FOMO(Fear of Missing Out) 증후군은 유행을 놓치거나 뒤처질 수 있다는 생각에 두려움을 느끼는 증후군이에요.
다음 중 해당하는 항목에 체크해보며 여러분도 FOMO 증후군이 있는지 확인해보세요. ☑

☐ 친구들이 SNS에 새로운 것을 배우거나 경험했다는 글을 올리면 마음이 불안해진다.
☐ SNS에 친구들보다 내가 먼저 새로운 정보를 올려야 마음이 편하다.
☐ 유명인과 친구를 맺고 자주 그 사람의 소식을 공유하려고 한다.
☐ 좋은 것을 보거나 먹기 전에 꼭 사진을 찍어 SNS에 올린다.

1 What is the best title for the passage?

① Having Trouble Making a Decision

② How to Deal with Difficult Choices

③ Some Ways to Make Smart Decisions

④ Your Choice Can Affect Other People

⑤ Wrong Choices Are Better than Nothing

2 What is the best order for sentences (A)~(C)?

① (A) – (B) – (C)　　　② (A) – (C) – (B)　　　③ (B) – (A) – (C)

④ (B) – (C) – (A)　　　⑤ (C) – (A) – (B)

3 Which is the best choice for the blank?

① they get more stressed

② they have enough information

③ they make fewer bad choices

④ they have to cancel their decisions

⑤ they can't get help from others

4 Which is the best choice to complete the sentence?

The best restaurant for people who have Hamlet Syndrome _____ .

① has many regular customers　　② sells food for a low price

③ has a pleasant atmosphere　　　④ serves only one dish

⑤ cooks food very quickly

Words

line 명 대사; 선, 줄　delay 동 미루다　main character 주인공　face 동 직면하다　situation 명 상황　struggle 동 애쓰다　decision 명 결정
frequently 부 자주　condition 명 문제; 상태　syndrome 명 증후군　option 명 선택(지)　see A as B A를 B로 여기다　phenomenon 명 현상
opportunity 명 기회　so-called 형 흔히 ~이라 불리는, 이른바　whatever 명 아무거나 <문제> deal with 처리하다　cancel 동 취소하다
regular customer 단골손님　pleasant 형 즐거운　atmosphere 명 분위기; 대기, 공기　serve 동 제공하다　dish 명 요리, 접시

Review Test

[1-3] 보기의 관계와 같도록 빈칸에 들어갈 단어를 쓰시오.

> 보기   option : optional

1 _____ : wealthy

2 _____ : free

3 _____ : popular

[4-5] 다음 영영 풀이에 해당하는 단어는?

4 a small object produced by a plant that can grow into a new plant

① branch   ② seed   ③ leaf   ④ organ   ⑤ stem

5 the army or people of a country which enters and controls another country

① soldier   ② disaster   ③ invader   ④ customer   ⑤ merchant

[6-8] 다음 빈칸에 들어갈 단어를 보기에서 골라 쓰시오.

> 보기   force   delay   vision   signal   situation

6 Grace has to buy new glasses because her _____ is poor.

7 I don't want to go to sleep early, but my parents always _____ me to do so.

8 The brain sends a _____ to our stomach when we need food.

[9-10] 다음 밑줄 친 단어나 표현에 유의하여 각 문장의 해석을 쓰시오.

9 But what do these puppet shows <u>have to do with</u> independence?

→ _____

10 Interestingly, some restaurants <u>see</u> this phenomenon <u>as</u> an opportunity to attract more customers.

→ _____

내 손으로 만드는 동물원

누구나 즐길 수 있는 그림자놀이

불빛과 벽만 있다면 어디서든 즐길 수 있는 그림자놀이!
쉬운 단계부터 고난도까지 다양한 그림자놀이를 여러분에게 선보입니다.
여러분들도 한번 그림자놀이의 고수가 되어보세요!

▶ 그림자놀이 하수

비둘기

개

거위

▶ 그림자놀이 중수

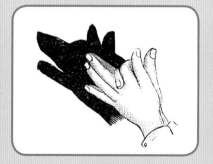

늑대

낙타

돼지

▶ 그림자놀이 고수

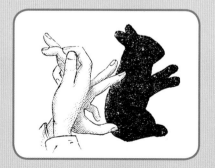

토끼

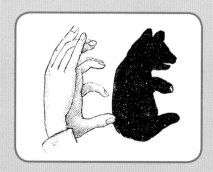

곰

염소

HackersBook.com

UNIT 05

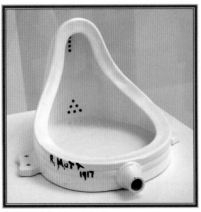
▲ *Fountain* by Marcel Duchamp

Have you ever seen a toilet exhibited as art? In 1917, Marcel Duchamp created a work called *Fountain*. The piece was just a common *urinal, but he turned it upside down to make it look like a fountain. This challenged many people's idea of what art could be. And it showed that _____ objects could be art as long as they were modified in a creative way.

A century later, another artist named Maurizio Cattelan created a sculpture in the form of a toilet, too. It was placed in a museum bathroom, and people could actually use it. More surprisingly, the sculpture was made entirely of gold!

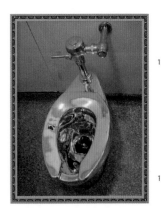
▲ *America* by Maurizio Cattelan

Cattelan named it *America*. Through *America*, he tried to criticize those who waste money on unnecessary objects. He also made people ask themselves whether they really desired overly luxurious things, like the golden toilet.

*urinal (남성용) 소변기

Read & Learn 황금 변기 <아메리카> 도난 사건!

2019년 9월, 영국 블레넘궁에서 황금 변기 <아메리카>의 도난 사건이 벌어졌습니다! 총 103kg의 금이 사용된 <아메리카>의 가치는 약 70억 원에 달하는데요. 경찰 수사 후 유력 용의자를 체포했으나, 여전히 도난품은 회수되지 못하고 있습니다. 전문가들은 범인이 <아메리카>를 훔친 지 24시간 이내에 금을 녹여 이미 팔았을 것이라고 예상합니다.

1 이 글의 목적으로 가장 적절한 것은?

① 예술 작품을 관람하는 올바른 태도를 안내하기 위해

② 유명한 예술 작품에 대한 새로운 해석을 제시하기 위해

③ 현대 예술에 영향을 미친 과거의 예술가들을 알리기 위해

④ 과거의 예술가들이 작품을 창작했던 과정을 설명하기 위해

⑤ 고정관념에서 벗어난 예술 작품과 그 의미를 소개하기 위해

2 이 글의 빈칸에 들어갈 말로 가장 적절한 것은?

① beautiful　　　② ordinary　　　③ historical

④ religious　　　⑤ heavy

3 이 글을 읽고 답할 수 <u>없는</u> 질문은?

① When was *Fountain* created?

② What was *Fountain* made of?

③ Where was *America* displayed?

④ What does the name of *America* mean?

⑤ Why did the artist make *America*?

4 이 글의 내용으로 보아, 다음 빈칸에 들어갈 말을 보기 에서 골라 쓰시오.

| 보기 | challenged | desired | criticized | luxurious | significant |

While *Fountain* _____ people's old idea of art, *America* _____ the unnecessary spending of money on _____ items.

Words

toilet 몡 변기　exhibit 통 전시하다　fountain 몡 샘, 분수　upside down (위아래가) 거꾸로　challenge 통 이의를 제기하다; 도전하다
object 몡 사물　as long as ~하기만 하면, ~하는 한　modify 통 바꾸다, 수정하다　century 몡 세기, 100년　sculpture 몡 조각상
entirely 빈 전부, 완전히　criticize 통 비판하다　desire 통 원하다 몡 욕망　overly 빈 지나치게, 몹시　luxurious 혱 사치스러운
golden 혱 금으로 된　<문제> ordinary 혱 일반적인　religious 혱 종교적인　display 통 전시하다　spending 몡 소비, 지출

Nowadays, many kids are creating videos and posting ⓐ <u>them</u> online. Many of ⓑ <u>their</u> videos become popular, and some even get millions of hits. Unfortunately, people sometimes post hateful comments about these videos. That's why a few websites have banned leaving comments for all videos posted by children. What do you think about this?

Andrew

Although these comments could be just jokes, young kids can be hurt by ⓒ <u>them</u> much more easily than adults. As a result, they can become discouraged and have lower self-esteem. In extreme cases, ⓓ <u>they</u> may even experience depression.

Not everyone posts hateful comments. Most of the comments are not harmful, and many are even encouraging. Banning all comments stops us from giving positive feedback. For kids, this means they lose the opportunity _____.

It is difficult for ⓔ <u>them</u> to know what people like or how to make their videos better.

Emma

1 이 글의 토론 주제로 가장 적절한 것은?

① 아이들이 제작하는 영상의 내용을 제한해야 하는가

② 아이들이 볼 수 있는 영상을 법으로 규제해야 하는가

③ 온라인 영상에 대한 댓글을 실명으로 남겨야 하는가

④ 온라인 영상을 제작할 수 있는 나이를 제한해야 하는가

⑤ 아이들이 올린 영상에 댓글을 남기는 것을 금지해야 하는가

2 이 글의 밑줄 친 ⓐ~ⓔ 중, 가리키는 대상이 같은 것끼리 짝지어진 것은?

① ⓐ, ⓑ　　　　② ⓐ, ⓓ　　　　③ ⓑ, ⓒ

④ ⓑ, ⓔ　　　　⑤ ⓒ, ⓔ

3 이 글의 빈칸에 들어갈 말로 가장 적절한 것은?

① to show their creativity　　② to make more videos

③ to realize their popularity　　④ to improve their content

⑤ to access the Internet

● 심화형

4 다음 중, Emma의 의견에 동의하는 사람을 <u>모두</u> 고른 것은?

Ellen

Comments can have a long-term negative impact on kids.

Sam

I think banning all comments would prevent people from saying positive things.

Tina

Comments provide video creators with useful feedback.

Lucas

The Internet needs to be a productive place, so we should ban mean comments.

① Ellen, Sam　　② Ellen, Lucas　　③ Sam, Tina

④ Sam, Lucas　　⑤ Tina, Lucas

Words

post 图 올리다 圄 우편　hit 圄 조회 수 图 때리다, 치다　hateful 圏 악의적인, 해로운　comment 圄 댓글　ban 图 금지하다　adult 圄 성인, 어른
discouraged 圏 좌절한, 낙담한　self-esteem 圄 자존감　depression 圄 우울증　encouraging 圏 힘을 북돋아 주는
positive 圏 긍정적인 (negative 圏 부정적인)　feedback 圄 피드백, 의견　<문제> improve 图 개선하다　access 图 접속하다 圄 접근
long-term 圏 장기적인　impact 圄 영향　productive 圏 생산적인　mean 圏 못된

Dr. James Barry was a famous British surgeon who served in the army in the 19th century. He made many professional contributions during his career.

(A) She got her degree in 1812, and she joined the army as a doctor the next year. She eventually became the second-highest medical officer in the army. Her life shows that women are just as capable as men.

(B) James Barry was originally Margaret Bulkley. She wanted to become a doctor, but women were not allowed to study medicine at the time. However, Bulkley would not give up her dream. She took her dead uncle's name and dressed up like a man. Then she entered the University of Edinburgh Medical School.

(C) One of them was promoting the importance of *sanitation in hospitals. For his entire professional life, however, he kept a great secret. After his death, it was revealed that Dr. James Barry was not a man but a woman!

*sanitation 공중위생

1 이 글의 단락 (A)~(C)를 순서에 맞게 배열한 것으로 가장 적절한 것은?

① (A) – (C) – (B)　　　　② (B) – (A) – (C)

③ (B) – (C) – (A)　　　　④ (C) – (A) – (B)

⑤ (C) – (B) – (A)

（심화형）

2 이 글의 내용과 가장 잘 어울리는 속담은?

① Look before you leap.

② Practice makes perfect.

③ Birds of a feather flock together.

④ Where there is a will, there is a way.

⑤ A little knowledge is a dangerous thing.

（서술형）

3 이 글의 밑줄 친 a great secret이 의미하는 내용을 우리말로 쓰시오.

_____

4 Margaret Bulkley의 생애를 다음과 같이 나타낼 때, 빈칸에 들어갈 말을 글에서 찾아 쓰시오.

> She used her uncle's (1) _____ to study (2) _____.

⌄

> After she got her degree, she worked in the (3) _____.

⌄

> She made many (4) _____ during her career as a doctor.

Words

surgeon 몡외과 의사　serve 동복무하다; 시중을 들다　army 몡군대　make a contribution 공을 세우다　professional 휑직업적인

career 몡경력　degree 몡학위　medical officer 군의관　capable 휑유능한, 할 수 있는　originally 뷔원래　medicine 몡의학

give up 포기하다　dress up 옷을 입다, 변장하다　promote 동알리다, 홍보하다　reveal 동밝히다, 드러내다　<문제> leap 동뛰다, 도약하다

feather 몡날개, 깃털　flock 동모이다　will 몡뜻, 의지　knowledge 몡지식

In the board game *Pandemic*, players must cooperate rather than compete. Each player picks a role, and everyone has to work together to prevent four diseases from spreading across the world.

When real pandemics occur, countries around the world react in the same way. (a) A pandemic is a disease that spreads across different regions of the world and infects a large proportion of the population. (b) Most pandemics originate from viruses that infect both animals and humans. (c) One example is the **swine flu. (d) It was declared a pandemic by the World Health Organization (WHO) in 2009. (e) After that, countries cooperated to share information about the virus and develop a vaccine. This allowed doctors around the world to treat patients quickly and effectively. Recently, countries have battled the worldwide coronavirus disease-2019 (COVID-19). Just like in the game, the entire world has put its differences aside to fight the pandemic.

*pandemic 팬데믹 (전 세계적인 유행병) **swine flu 돼지 독감 (신종 인플루엔자)

Read & Learn

Pandemic의 'demic'은 '사람들, 지역'을 뜻하는 그리스어로, demic으로 끝나는 단어들은 대부분 전염병, 바이러스와 관련이 있어요. demic으로 끝나는 단어에 무엇이 있는지 알아볼까요?

endemic en(안에, 내에) + demic(사람들, 지역)	epidemic epi(사이에) + demic(사람들, 지역)	pandemic pan(모든) + demic(사람들, 지역)
몡 (특정 지역 또는 집단에서 나타나는) 풍토병	몡 (한 지역에서 갑자기 빠르게 퍼지는) 유행성 전염병	몡 (한 나라나 대륙, 전 세계와 같이 아주 넓은 지역에서 퍼지는) 유행병

1 What is the best title for the passage?

① Pandemics: Bringing People Together

② Serious Damage Caused by Pandemics

③ A Worldwide Popularity of a Board Game

④ How Can We Prevent Widespread Diseases?

⑤ Achievements of the World Health Organization

2 Among (a)~(e), which is the best answer for the question?

Q. What is the main cause of a pandemic?

① (a)　　　② (b)　　　③ (c)　　　④ (d)　　　⑤ (e)

(서술형)

3 How did countries fight the swine flu? Write the answer in Korean.

_____

4 Complete the sentences with the following words.

battling	pandemic	vaccine	spreading

Coronavirus Outbreak

On 11 March 2020, the WHO declared coronavirus disease-2019 a
_____. It infected a lot of people, and many countries tried to
keep it from _____ across the world.

Words

cooperate 통 협력하다 rather than ~보다는 compete 통 경쟁하다 occur 통 발생하다 react 통 대응하다, 반응하다 region 명 지역
infect 통 감염시키다 proportion 명 비율, 부분 population 명 인구 originate from ~에서 비롯되다 virus 명 바이러스 declare 통 선언하다
organization 명 기구, 조직, 단체 vaccine 명 백신 effectively 부 효과적으로 battle 통 싸우다 put aside ~을 제쳐두다
<문제> bring ~ together ~를 (한데) 모이게 하다 widespread 형 널리 퍼진 achievement 명 업적, 성취 outbreak 명 발생, 발발

Review Test

정답 및 해설 p.86

1 단어의 성격이 나머지와 <u>다른</u> 것은?

① pleasant   ② nutrient   ③ adult   ④ scent   ⑤ accident

2 다음 중, 단어의 영영 풀이가 올바르지 <u>않은</u> 것은?

① sculpture - an artwork that someone made out of a material like stone or wood
② region - the belief in a god or gods
③ achievement - a good result gained by hard work
④ population - the total number of people who live in a particular area
⑤ access - a way of approaching or getting close to something or someone

3 다음 밑줄 친 단어와 가장 비슷한 의미의 단어는?

The critics <u>declared</u> that *Dracula* was the best film of the year.

① reviewed   ② desired   ③ announced   ④ challenged   ⑤ occurred

[4-8] 다음 빈칸에 들어갈 단어나 표현을 보기에서 골라 쓰시오.

보기	as long as criticize put aside rather than promote

4 I can still watch the TV show _____ I get home by eight o'clock.

5 The store started to _____ its opening event.

6 I will continue studying hard for the exam _____ give up.

7 Let's _____ the problems and talk about the good things first.

8 The public _____d the factory because it polluted the lake.

[9-10] 다음 밑줄 친 단어나 표현에 유의하여 각 문장의 해석을 쓰시오.

9 He <u>made</u> many professional <u>contributions</u> during his career.

→ _____

10 Most pandemics <u>originate from</u> viruses that infect both animals and humans.

→ _____

작심삼일은 그만! 매일 할 수 있는
간단한 홈트레이닝

방 안에서 매일 할 수 있는 간단하면서 쉬운 '홈트레이닝' 동작들을 소개합니다!
방 안에서 매일 할 수 있는 간단하면서 쉬운 '홈트레이닝' 동작들을 소개합니다!
지금 일어나서 함께 따라 해볼까요? Let's go!

골반교정에 좋은
백 런지

❸ 무릎이 닿기 전까지 내려간 뒤
시작 자세로 천천히 돌아와요.

⚠ **주의!**
앞쪽 무릎이 발끝보다 앞으로 나아가면
무릎이 아플 수 있으니 주의하세요!

❷ 한쪽 다리를 뒤로 뻗어요.

❶ 옆에서 보았을 때 척추부터 발끝까지
일직선이 되도록 바르게 서요.

튼튼한 등 만들기
슈퍼맨 풀다운

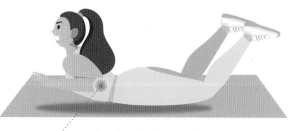

❶ 엎드린 자세에서 팔은 앞으로 뻗고 다리는
어깨너비로 벌려요.

❷ 팔꿈치를 최대한 몸 가까이 수직으로 당겨 W자를
만들면서 상체와 다리를 동시에 들어 올려요.

⚠ **주의!**
앞 팔을 수직으로 당길 때 팔꿈치가 손목보다
위로 올라가지 않도록 해야 해요!

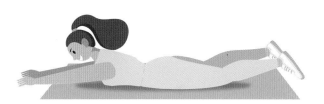

HackersBook.com

UNIT 06

During my homestay in Germany, my host's cousin Karl had a wedding. I was invited to his house for a party the night before the wedding. Karl told me to bring some plates. 3 It was a little odd, but I thought he needed extra plates for all the guests.

However, once the party started, everyone gathered 6 together and suddenly threw their dishes on the ground! The ground became a mess, but everyone was smiling happily. 9

I asked one of the guests why everyone was breaking the plates. He said, "To wish the couple good luck in their marriage." This event is called *Polterabend*, a wedding 12 tradition in Germany. Germans do this because of the old saying, "*Shards bring luck."

"But don't break a mirror," the guest said. "That means 15 seven years of bad luck!"

*shard 조각, 파편

1 이 글의 주제로 가장 적절한 것은?

① an unusual wedding tradition

② plates as a popular wedding gift

③ a special place to have a wedding

④ how Germans treat guests at parties

⑤ traditional table manners in Germany

2 이 글의 밑줄 친 I가 파티 시작 직후에 느꼈을 심경으로 가장 적절한 것은?

① annoyed　　　　② bored　　　　③ confused

④ pleased　　　　⑤ disappointed

3 다음 질문에 대한 답이 되도록 빈칸에 들어갈 말을 글에서 찾아 쓰시오.

> Q. What do Germans think about breaking plates and mirrors?

> A. They think breaking plates brings ＿＿＿＿＿＿ ＿＿＿＿＿＿,
>   while breaking mirrors brings ＿＿＿＿＿＿ ＿＿＿＿＿＿.

4 이 글의 내용과 일치하도록 (A)~(D)를 알맞은 순서대로 배열하시오.

> (A) I was told to bring some plates to a party.
>
> (B) I learned about a German tradition called *Polterabend*.
>
> (C) A party to celebrate the wedding began.
>
> (D) Everyone made the ground a mess.

＿＿＿＿＿ ➡ ＿＿＿＿＿ ➡ ＿＿＿＿＿ ➡ ＿＿＿＿＿

Words

homestay 명 홈스테이(유학 등의 이유로 외국으로 떠났을 때 해당 지역의 외국인 가정집에서 지내는 것) cousin 명 사촌
have a wedding 결혼식을 올리다[치르다] plate 명 접시 odd 형 이상한 extra 형 여분의 gather 동 모이다, 모으다 mess 명 난장판
break 동 부수다, 깨다 marriage 명 결혼 생활, 결혼 tradition 명 전통 (traditional 형 전통적인) old saying 옛말, 속담 (saying 명 속담, 격언)
<문제> manners 명 예절; (단수형) 방식 annoyed 형 짜증이 난 confused 형 혼란스러운 pleased 형 기쁜 disappointed 형 실망한

*Viral marketing is a powerful advertising tool. The term *viral* refers to the way product information spreads quickly and widely, like the way a virus infects people.

The Daily Twist campaign by Oreo cookies is a good example of this. In honor of its 100-year anniversary, the company started a new promotion. It revealed a fun image of an Oreo inspired by pop culture once a day for 100 days. From June 25 to October 2, the images were posted on its social media pages. For example, a "Batman Oreo" image was posted when *The Dark Knight Rises* movie came out. There was also a "Gangnam Style Oreo" that showed the famous horse dance.

The campaign was a huge success. Within three days, the images got 26 million "likes." Though Oreo didn't ask people to share the event, the images were all over social media, spreading as fast as a _____!

*viral marketing 바이럴 마케팅 (SNS 등을 이용한 상품 판매 전략)

1 이 글의 목적으로 가장 적절한 것은?

① to recommend some useful social media sites

② to explain the effects of social media on people

③ to describe how companies develop new products

④ to compare different types of marketing strategies

⑤ to introduce a successful example of viral marketing

2 이 글에 따르면, 오레오 쿠키가 100주년을 기념하기 위해 한 일은?

① 신제품을 개발하여 광고했다.

② 대형 쿠키 모형을 제작했다.

③ 다양한 쿠키 사진을 공개했다.

④ 쿠키 제작 과정의 변천사를 선보였다.

⑤ 소셜 미디어 페이지를 개설했다.

3 이 글의 내용과 일치하면 T, 그렇지 않으면 F를 쓰시오.

(1) Viral marketing allows product information to spread quickly.

(2) Oreo cookies encouraged people to share ideas for its Daily Twist campaign.

(3) The Daily Twist campaign lasted 100 days and ended successfully.

(심화형)

4 이 글의 빈칸에 들어갈 말을 글에서 찾아 쓰시오.

_____

Words

advertising 명 광고 **tool** 명 수단, 도구 **term** 명 용어 **viral** 형 바이러스성의 (**virus** 명 바이러스) **refer to** ~을 나타내다, 가리키다
infect 동 감염시키다 **campaign** 명 캠페인, 광고 **in honor of** ~을 기념하여 **anniversary** 명 주년, 기념일 **promotion** 명 홍보 (활동)
reveal 동 공개하다, 밝히다 **inspire** 동 영감을 주다 **pop culture** 대중문화 <문제> **recommend** 동 추천하다 **describe** 동 설명하다, 묘사하다
compare 동 비교하다 **strategy** 명 전략 **introduce** 동 소개하다 **encourage** 동 장려하다

Most people hate sweating because it makes them smell bad and feel sticky. However, sweat can tell us a lot about our bodies. And now, sweat sensors are taking advantage of it.

A sweat sensor is a patch that is small, thin, and flexible. You stick it on your body, and it measures specific chemicals in your sweat. For example, it can show *glucose levels. This is

▲ 스티커형 땀 센서

particularly _____ to those with diabetes. Without it, they have to get multiple blood tests throughout the day just to check their glucose levels. It can even help people predict heart attacks by checking the **potassium levels in their sweat.

Sweat sensors are able to reduce the time and effort required to check certain health conditions. They can even make it possible to monitor the physical conditions in real time. And best of all, they are comfortable to wear!

*glucose 포도당   **potassium 칼륨[포타슘]

1 이 글의 제목으로 가장 적절한 것은?

① A Convenient Way to Check Your Health

② The More You Sweat, the Better You Feel

③ What Happens in Your Body When You Sweat?

④ Wearable Devices That Help Reduce Sweating

⑤ Sweat Sensors: A Tool to Detect Body Movements

 서술형

2 이 글의 밑줄 친 it이 의미하는 내용을 우리말로 쓰시오.

_____

3 이 글의 빈칸에 들어갈 말로 가장 적절한 것은?

① light   ② useful   ③ familiar

④ expensive   ⑤ sensitive

4 땀 센서에 관한 이 글의 내용과 일치하지 <u>않는</u> 것은?

① 얇고 신축성이 있다.

② 땀의 양과 냄새를 분석한다.

③ 포도당 수치를 측정할 수 있다.

④ 심장마비를 예측할 수 있다.

⑤ 실시간으로 몸 상태를 파악할 수 있다.

Words

sweat 통땀 흘리다 명땀   sticky 형끈적거리는   take advantage of (기회 등을) 이용하다   patch 명패치, 천 조각   flexible 형탄력 있는
stick 통붙이다   measure 통측정하다   specific 형특정한, 구체적인   chemical 명화학 성분[물질]   level 명수치, 수준   particularly 부특히
diabetes 명당뇨   multiple 형다수의, 복수의   predict 통예측하다   heart attack 심장마비   reduce 통줄이다
monitor 통확인하다; 관찰[감시]하다   physical 형몸의, 신체의; 물리적인   in real time 실시간으로   comfortable 형편한
<문제> convenient 형편리한   wearable device 웨어러블[착용형] 기기   detect 통감지하다   familiar 형친숙한   sensitive 형민감한

Here's a personality test. Check the box if the statement applies to you.

☐ You have a need for others to like and admire you. ₃

☐ You sometimes doubt if you have made the right decision.

☐ You are often too critical of yourself. ₆

☐ Sometimes you are outgoing, but other times you are shy.

How many boxes did you check? If you checked all four of them, you've just experienced the Barnum Effect. It refers ₉ to our tendency to believe that personality descriptions are accurate and apply specifically to us. This psychological effect happens because the descriptions sound specific, but ₁₂ only on the surface. If we take a closer look, we discover they are so vague and general that they can apply to everyone. In fact, personality tests, *horoscopes, and fortune cookies all ₁₅ use the Barnum Effect.

Try it out on your friends. Show the statements to each friend individually. They will probably all say ₁₈

_____!

*horoscope 점성술, 별자리 운세

Read & Learn | 뻔한 심리테스트가 질린다면, 책으로 점을 쳐보는 건 어떤가요?

bibliomancy(책점)
: 책(biblio)을 펼쳐서 나오는 페이지에 있는 문구로 점(mancy)을 침

방법:
1. 점을 칠 책 한 권을 고르세요. 진리를 담고 있다고 믿는 책이면 더욱 좋습니다.

2. 묻고 싶은 질문을 생각하며 책을 펼친 후 그대로 바닥을 향해 떨어뜨립니다.

3. 눈을 감은 채 펼쳐진 페이지에서 아무 구절 이나 손가락으로 짚습니다.

4. 이 선택된 구절이 바로 질문에 대한 해답 입니다!

1 Choose ALL that are mentioned about the Barnum Effect in the passage.

① its strengths and weaknesses

② the reason why it occurs

③ its opposite effect

④ examples where it appears

⑤ the person who discovered it

2 Complete the conversation with a word from the passage.

A: I finished my painting, but it's not good.

B: It's fine. Don't be too _____ of yourself.

3 Which is the best choice for the blank?

① they've seen the statements before

② some statements need more details

③ the statements are relevant to their friends

④ the statements describe them perfectly

⑤ they cannot understand the statements

4 Complete the sentence with words from the passage.

It is easy to believe personality descriptions are _____
and _____ , but in fact, they are _____
and _____ .

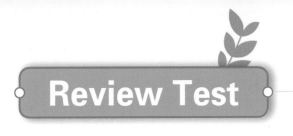

Review Test

정답 및 해설 p.87

1 짝지어진 단어의 관계가 나머지와 <u>다른</u> 것은?

① gather – collect   ② reveal – show   ③ describe – explain

④ specific – vague   ⑤ comfortable – convenient

[2-3] 다음 영영 풀이에 해당하는 단어는?

2   to say that an event or situation will happen in the future

① predict   ② admire   ③ detect   ④ inspire   ⑤ recommend

3   a detailed plan or method to achieve success

① promotion   ② mess   ③ equipment   ④ strategy   ⑤ statement

[4-6] 다음 빈칸에 들어갈 단어를 보기에서 골라 쓰시오.

보기	introduce	apply	doubt	measure	break

4   I _____ that Brad is telling me the truth because he looks nervous.

5   The new rules in professional basketball will _____ to every country.

6   We need to _____ the size of the desk before we put it in the room.

[7-8] 다음 빈칸에 들어갈 표현을 보기에서 골라 쓰시오.

보기	in honor of	fall out of	try out	be located in

7   I decided to _____ several products before choosing one.

8   _____ my parent's 20th wedding anniversary, I bought them flowers.

[9-10] 다음 밑줄 친 단어나 표현에 유의하여 각 문장의 해석을 쓰시오.

9   The term *viral* <u>refers to</u> the way product information spreads quickly and widely, like the way a virus infects people.

→ _____

10 And now, sweat sensors are <u>taking advantage of</u> it.

→ _____

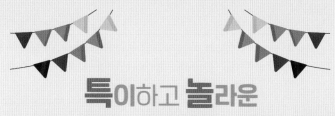

특이하고 놀라운
세계 결혼 문화
알아보기

우리나라의 결혼식에 고유한 문화와 풍습이 존재하듯, 나라마다 다양한 결혼 풍습이 있는데요.
세계 속 **이색적이고 독특한 결혼 문화!** 어떤 것들이 있는지 함께 알아볼까요?

 브라질

결혼하려면 시험을 봐야 한다고?

삼바와 열정의 나라 브라질! 결혼도 열정만 있으면 되는 줄 알았지만, 시험을 치러야
한다는 사실, 알고 있었나요? 결혼 전, 신랑과 신부는 일정 기간 전문기관에서 결혼
교육을 받게 되는데요. 교육을 마치면 시험을 치를 수 있는 자격이 주어져요. 시험에
합격하면 결혼을 할 수 있답니다! 열심히 공부했는데 시험에 떨어지면 어떻게 되냐고요?
물론, 떨어졌다고 해서 결혼을 절대 못 하는 것은 아니에요. 다만, 유산 상속 등 여러
가지에 있어 불이익이 있을 수 있다니 합격하는 게 더 좋겠죠?

 스코틀랜드

예비부부가 쓰레기 세례를 받는다?

스코틀랜드에서는 결혼식 며칠 전 밀가루, 날달걀, 썩은 우유 등의 오물을 뒤집어쓴 채로
동네를 행진하는 예비 신랑·신부의 모습을 볼 수 있는데요. 예비부부에게 각종 음식물
쓰레기 등을 퍼붓은 사람들은 다름 아닌, 바로 그들의 가족과 친한 친구들이랍니다. 아니,
이게 무슨 일일까요? 결혼식 전에 축복은커녕 쓰레기 세례라니! 스코틀랜드의 이러한
결혼 풍습은 액땜의 의미와 더불어, 결혼 생활을 함께할 부부에게 훗날 마주할 고난들을
잘 극복하라는 의미도 담겨 있다고 하네요.

HackersBook.com

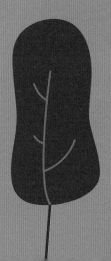

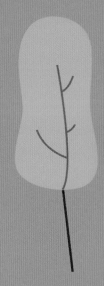

UNIT 07

Have you ever stood in line to buy a limited-edition product, such as Nike Air Max shoes? <u>Many people</u> wait in line for hours, and some even put up a tent in front of the store. Interestingly, none of these people (A) appreciate / complain . What makes them willing to spend such a long time waiting?

There are some products you can only buy for a short time or in limited numbers. They might be collaborations between brands and artists, or items that celebrities used to wear. These are very (B) ordinary / rare , and not everyone can buy them. Because people feel more satisfied once they get them, they don't mind waiting for these items.

Besides, waiting in line may not be so (C) good / bad . You and everyone else in the line share a <u>common</u> interest, so you can have a nice chat with them. You may even make a new friend!

● 심화형

1 이 글의 밑줄 친 Many people의 주장으로 가장 적절한 것은?

① "The value of some products decreases over time."

② "It is important to satisfy diverse customer tastes."

③ "The more people buy, the less pleased they are."

④ "Products that are hard to get can give more joy."

⑤ "People buy more when they have to wait in line."

2 (A), (B), (C)의 각 네모 안에서 문맥에 알맞은 말을 골라 쓰시오.

(A): _____   (B): _____   (C): _____

3 이 글의 밑줄 친 common과 같은 뜻으로 쓰인 것은?

① What is the most common blood type?

② A cold is one of the most common diseases.

③ The mango is a common fruit in the Philippines.

④ Buses and subways are common forms of transportation.

⑤ Sara and I are very similar and even have common hobbies.

4 이 글의 내용으로 보아, 다음 빈칸에 들어갈 말을 글에서 찾아 쓰시오.

> Some people are willing to _____ for a long time to get limited-edition items. They are _____ with their purchases because not everyone can have these items.

Words

limited-edition 형 한정판의 (limited 형 한정된) wait in line 줄을 서서 기다리다 put up ~을 치다, 세우다, 짓다 appreciate 동 감사하다
complain 동 불평하다 willing to 기꺼이 ~하는 collaboration 명 공동 제작품 celebrity 명 유명인
satisfied 형 만족한 (satisfy 동 만족시키다) mind 동 꺼리다 besides 부 게다가 common 형 공통의; 흔한 chat 명 대화
<문제> decrease 동 하락하다, 감소하다 diverse 형 다양한 taste 명 취향 joy 명 기쁨 blood type 혈액형 transportation 명 교통, 운송
purchase 명 구매

On his 66th birthday, William Reed was enjoying a party with his family. His wife told him, "ⓐ <u>I</u> have a present for you. Open it!" The gift looked like a pair of ordinary sunglasses. William put them on, and all of a sudden, everything around ⓑ <u>him</u> looked different! It was the first time that he was able to see color because William was color-blind. Until that moment, ⓒ <u>his</u> life had always been in black and white.

What changed ⓓ <u>his</u> world was a pair of special glasses made for color-blind people. The lenses are coated with a material that exaggerates certain *wavelengths of light. This makes colors look much richer and more vivid. That's why ⓔ <u>William</u> could distinguish different colors after putting on the glasses.

For now, these glasses don't work for all types of color blindness. Yet, they have helped many color-blind people experience a colorful world.

*wavelength 파장

Read & Learn

사람만 색맹이 있는 개 아니냥! 강아지와 고양이는 빨간색과 초록색을 구별하지 못하는 적록색맹이랍니다. 실제로, 신호등을 볼 때 강아지와 고양이의 눈에는 세 가지 색깔이 모두 노란색으로 보여요. 그렇다면 색맹을 결정 짓는 요인은 무엇일까요? 망막세포 안에는 색깔을 인식하는 역할을 하는 원추세포가 있는데, 색맹이 아닌 사람에게는 빨강, 노랑, 파랑 세 가지 색을 모두 인식할 수 있는 원추세포가 있어요. 그러나 강아지에게는 노랑과 파랑 두 가지의 색깔만 인식하는 원추세포가 있고, 고양이에게는 원추세포가 적게 있거나 아예 없답니다.

1 이 글의 주제로 가장 적절한 것은?

① how to improve your vision

② how color-blind glasses are made

③ characteristics of being color-blind

④ special glasses to help a color-blind man

⑤ why some people see things in black and white

2 이 글의 밑줄 친 ⓐ~ⓔ 중, 가리키는 대상이 나머지 넷과 <u>다른</u> 것은?

① ⓐ   ② ⓑ   ③ ⓒ   ④ ⓓ   ⑤ ⓔ

(서술형)

3 William이 선물을 착용한 후 어떤 변화가 있었는지 우리말로 쓰시오.

_____

4 특수 안경에 관한 이 글의 내용과 일치하면 T, 그렇지 않으면 F를 쓰시오.

(1) 렌즈에 빛의 특정 파장을 축소시키는 물질이 입혀져 있어 색을 더욱 진하고 선명하게 볼 수 있다. _____

(2) 현재로서는 색맹인 사람들 모두에게 효과가 있는 것은 아니다. _____

5 다음 영영 풀이에 해당하는 단어를 글에서 찾아 쓰시오.

> to tell the difference between two or more things

_____

Words

put on ~을 쓰다, 입다, 착용하다   **all of a sudden** 갑자기   **color-blind** 휑 색맹인 (**color blindness** 색맹)   **black and white** 흑백(의)
coat 통 칠하다, 입히다   **material** 몡 물질   **exaggerate** 통 과장하다   **rich** 휑 풍부한; 부유한   **vivid** 휑 선명한, 생생한   **distinguish** 통 구분하다
work 통 효과가 있다, 잘되다; 일하다   **colorful** 휑 형형색색의   <문제> **vision** 몡 시력   **characteristic** 몡 특징
tell the difference (차이를) 구별하다

Do you think your daily activities are interesting enough to share with the world? (A) GRWM (Get Ready With Me) is a popular type of vlog that shows a person getting ready ₃ for school, work, or an event. (B) Recently, many people have been recording their day-to-day lives and sharing the videos online. (C) These are called video blogs, or vlogs. ₆

Viewers sometimes ＿＿＿＿＿＿＿＿＿＿ through these videos. Some watch couples' vlogs to get ideas of where to go on a date. Others watch vlogs from chefs to ₉ learn cooking tips and recipes.

The most successful vlogs are usually made by celebrities. They often use vlogs to directly connect with their fans. They ₁₂ also show their real personalities in their daily lives through vlogs. This makes the content sound more sincere and gives fans the impression of having a personal relationship with ₁₅ them.

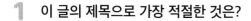

1 이 글의 제목으로 가장 적절한 것은?

① How to Make Your Own Vlog

② Sharing One's Daily Life in Videos

③ How to Enjoy Every Day of Your Life

④ Differences between Vlogs and Blogs

⑤ You Can Build a Personal Relationship Online

2 이 글의 문장 (A)~(C)를 순서에 맞게 배열한 것으로 가장 적절한 것은?

① (A) – (C) – (B)　　② (B) – (A) – (C)　　③ (B) – (C) – (A)

④ (C) – (A) – (B)　　⑤ (C) – (B) – (A)

3 이 글의 빈칸에 들어갈 말로 가장 적절한 것은?

① share some memories

② communicate with others

③ see many advertisements

④ receive tips for everyday life

⑤ relieve stress from daily life

4 이 글에서 브이로그에 관해 언급되지 <u>않은</u> 것은?

① what they are　　② contents of them

③ the benefits they offer　　④ why celebrities make them

⑤ the equipment to create them

You may have noticed that your tongue sometimes feels painful when you eat pineapple. Why does <u>this</u> happen? It's because pineapples contain an *enzyme that makes your mouth burn! But there is no need to worry. (a) It's too weak to do any serious damage. (b) And your mouth is capable of healing itself quickly. (c) Besides, this enzyme is what makes pineapple helpful. (d) It breaks down the protein in the food we eat, which makes it easier to digest. (e) Getting the right amount of protein in your diet is good for your health. For this reason, pineapple is often served with dishes that contain lots of protein, such as beef or pork.

Pineapples are not the only fruit with this enzyme. Many other fruits like kiwis and mangoes have it, and they cause a stinging feeling, too!

*enzyme 효소

Read & Learn

파인애플의 원래 이름은 '파인애플'이 아니다?

파인애플은 원산지인 남미를 비롯해 대부분의 나라에서 '아나나스(Ananas)'라고 불려요. 하지만 미대륙을 탐험하던 한 영국인이 파인애플을 보고는 솔방울(pine cone)과 닮았지만 맛은 사과(apple)처럼 달다는 의미에서 '파인애플'이라는 이름을 지었고, 이 이름이 알려지며 영어권 국가와 한국, 중국, 일본에서는 '파인애플'이라고 부르게 되었다고 해요.

1 What is the main topic of the passage?

① common nutrients in fruits and meats

② problems caused by pineapple allergies

③ special enzymes found only in pineapple

④ how an enzyme in pineapples affects your body

⑤ why the tongue is the most sensitive body part

(서술형)

2 What does the underlined this mean in the passage? Write the answer in Korean.

_____

3 Among (a)~(e), which sentence does NOT fit in the context?

① (a)   ② (b)   ③ (c)   ④ (d)   ⑤ (e)

4 Complete the answer with words from the passage.

> Q. Why is pineapple often served with beef or pork?

A. To help to _____ the meat by breaking down the _____ in it

5 Complete each sentence with ONE word from the passage.

> • I fell off my bicycle but had no _____ injuries.
> • Edward is a _____ person who does not laugh often.

Words

tongue 명 혀 painful 형 아픈, 고통스러운 burn 동 화끈거리다; 타다 serious 형 심각한; 진지한 damage 명 손상, 피해
be capable of ~할 수 있다 heal 동 치유하다 break down 분해하다 protein 명 단백질 digest 동 소화하다 diet 명 식단 dish 명 요리; 접시
beef 명 소고기 pork 명 돼지고기 stinging 형 찌르는 듯한 <문제> nutrient 명 영양소 allergy 명 알레르기 injury 명 부상

UNIT 07 | 87

UNIT 07
4

Hackers Reading Smart Level 3

[1-3] 다음 밑줄 친 단어와 가장 비슷한 의미의 단어를 알맞게 연결하시오.

1 Eating too much junk food causes <u>damage</u> to your stomach. •

• ⓐ conversation

2 Please accept my <u>sincere</u> apology for what happened yesterday. •

• ⓑ truthful

3 The teacher had a <u>chat</u> with my parents about my grades. •

• ⓒ harm

[4-6] 다음 괄호 안에서 알맞은 단어를 골라 표시하시오.

4 Many guests of the hotel (complained / promised) about the dirty rooms.

5 I don't (remind / mind) sharing food with my friends.

6 Reading books has many (benefits / proteins), like improving your thinking skills.

[7-8] 자연스러운 대화가 되도록 빈칸에 들어갈 단어를 보기 에서 골라 쓰시오.

보기	personality	recipe	purchase	content

7 A: Do you know how to make spaghetti sauce?

B: Let me search for the _____ on the Internet.

8 A: What did you think of your science class?

B: It was difficult, but the _____ was fascinating.

[9-10] 다음 밑줄 친 단어나 표현에 유의하여 각 문장의 해석을 쓰시오.

9 What makes them <u>willing</u> to spend such a long time waiting?

→ _____

10 And your mouth <u>is capable of</u> healing itself quickly.

→ _____

손쉽게 뚝딱!
누구나 만들 수 있는 초간단 브런치

과일을 더 맛있게 즐길 수 있는 쉽고 간단한 브런치 레시피를 소개할게요!

상큼 달달
딸기 롤 샌드위치

준비물 : 식빵, 딸기(또는 바나나, 키위 등 다른 과일도 가능), 크림치즈, 밀대

만드는 방법

STEP 1 흐르는 물에 딸기를 깨끗하게 씻은 후 물기와 꼭지를 제거해요.

STEP 2 맛과 멋을 위해 식빵의 가장자리를 자르고, 밀대로 납작하게 밀어요.

STEP 3 식빵에 크림치즈를 바르고 그 위에 딸기를 올린 후 돌돌 말아요.

STEP 4 돌돌 만 식빵을 먹기 좋은 크기로 잘라주면 딸기 롤 샌드위치 만들기 끝!

TIP 롤 샌드위치를 자를 때, 딸기의 가장 통통한 부분을 잘라야 모양도 예쁘고 딸기가 빠지지 않아요!

고소함 가득
아보카도 토스트

준비물 : 식빵, 슬라이스 치즈, 아보카도, 베이컨, 후추

만드는 방법

STEP 1 달궈진 팬에 베이컨을 구워요.

STEP 2 식빵을 구운 후, 그 위에 베이컨과 슬라이스 치즈를 올려요.

STEP 3 아보카도를 반으로 자른 후, 얇게 썰어주고 살짝 구워줘요.

STEP 4 베이컨과 치즈가 올려진 빵 위에 구워놓은 아보카도를 올려주고 후추로 간을 해주면 끝!

 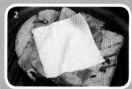 

TIP 집에 달걀이 있다면 반숙으로 익혀서 아보카도 위에 올려보세요. 노른자를 터트려 함께 먹으면 고소한 맛이 두 배가 돼요!

HackersBook.com

UNIT 08

Aladdin and the Magic Lamp is a popular story of an Arabian character named Aladdin. In many books and movies, the story takes place in the Middle East. However, in the original book, the story is set somewhere in China! How did two very different cultures appear in one old story, then? It might be because of the Silk Road.

The Silk Road was a network of ancient trade routes. This 6,400-kilometer-long road _____. Chinese merchants sold various kinds of goods, including tea and silk, along the routes to the Middle East and Rome. Silk was the most popular item, so it became the road's name. In addition to merchandise, Chinese traders also shared various other things, like their food and fables. As a result of this cultural exchange, stories like Aladdin's developed.

1 이 글의 빈칸에 들어갈 말로 가장 적절한 것은?

① was closed for a long time

② became a symbol of the West

③ protected China from other countries

④ was built over a long period of time

⑤ connected China to countries in the West

2 이 글의 내용과 일치하도록 괄호 안에서 알맞은 말을 골라 표시하시오.

> The original story of *Aladdin and the Magic Lamp* takes places in
> (1) (China / the Middle East), even though most media say it happens in
> (2) (China / the Middle East).

3 이 글을 읽고 비단길에 관해 답할 수 <u>없는</u> 질문은?

① How long was it?　　　　　② How many routes did it include?

③ How did it get its name?　　④ How did it affect the story of Aladdin?

⑤ What was exchanged through it?

4 이 글의 내용으로 보아, 빈칸 (A)와 (B)에 들어갈 말로 가장 적절한 것은?

> Chinese merchants _____(A)_____ goods with people from other countries
> along the Silk Road. They _____(B)_____ culture along with merchandise,
> which resulted in stories like *Aladdin and the Magic Lamp*.

	(A)		(B)		(A)		(B)
①	developed	······	changed	②	developed	······	experienced
③	traded	······	exchanged	④	traded	······	separated
⑤	exchanged	······	separated				

Words

Arabian 몡아랍인 톙아랍의　**take place** 일어나다, 발생하다　**Middle East** 중동　**set** 툉(연극·영화 등의) 배경을 설정하다; 놓다 (**set-set-set**)
appear 툉나타나다; ~처럼 보이다　**silk** 몡비단, 실크　**network** 몡연결망　**trade** 몡무역, 거래 툉거래하다, 무역하다 (**trader** 몡상인)
route 몡경로　**merchant** 몡상인 (**merchandise** 몡상품)　**goods** 몡상품, 물건; (단수형) 선, 좋은 것　**fable** 몡우화
exchange 몡교류, 교환 툉교류하다, 교환하다　**develop** 툉생기다; 개발하다　<문제> **symbol** 몡상징　**result in** (결과적으로) ~을 낳다
separate 툉분리하다

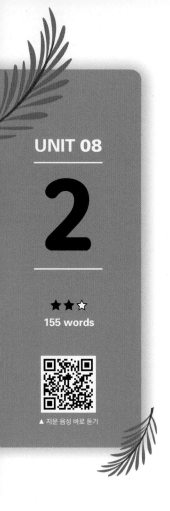
Valley Curtain was a work by the artists Christo and Jeanne-Claude. It was a 381-meter-long wall of orange cloth hanging between two Colorado mountain slopes. It looked like a curtain laid down by a giant. (①) For 28 months between 1970 and 1972, they sketched the curtain's shape, dyed a huge piece of fabric, and found a suitable valley. (②) However, the work was destroyed by strong winds, just 28 hours after it was installed. (③) They had to remove the work, but they were not frustrated. (④) In fact, this was close to what they expected! (⑤)

This style of artwork is known as *land art or Earth art. Land artists want their work to be a part of nature. *Valley Curtain*, for example, swayed as the wind blew, so it changed with the movement of nature. In the end, it was also finished by nature.

*land art(= Earth art) 대지 미술

▼ *Valley Curtain* by Christo and Jeanne-Claude

1 이 글의 주제로 가장 적절한 것은?

① an effort to protect nature

② engineers who became artists

③ artwork created within nature

④ a valley that looks like a curtain

⑤ a challenge to fight climate change

2 이 글의 흐름으로 보아, 다음 문장이 들어가기에 가장 적절한 곳은?

> Then, they gathered a team of 100 engineers and installed the curtain.

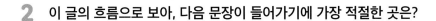

①   ②   ③   ④   ⑤

• 심화형

3 *Valley Curtain*의 제작 의도를 가장 잘 파악한 사람은?

① 지현: 모든 작품의 가치는 영원할 수 없어.

② 명수: 작품이 자연의 일부가 되어 변화하고 있어.

③ 수민: 거대한 자연 앞에서 인간은 나약한 존재야.

④ 준하: 우리가 보호해야 할 자연의 모습을 본떠 만들어졌어.

⑤ 민경: 한 작품을 만들기 위해서는 많은 시간과 정성을 들여야 해.

4 *Valley Curtain*에 관한 이 글의 내용과 일치하지 <u>않는</u> 것은?

Location	① It was installed between two mountain slopes.
Production Method	② It was made by dying a giant cloth.
Aspects	③ The display period was shorter than the production period. ④ It could withstand strong winds. ⑤ It is an example of land art.

Words

valley 몡계곡 curtain 몡커튼 cloth 몡천; (복수형) 옷 hang 통걸리다, 걸다 mountain slope 산비탈 lay 통놓다; (알을) 낳다 (lay-laid-laid)
sketch 통~의 밑그림을 그리다 dye 통염색하다 fabric 몡천 suitable 혱적절한 destroy 통파괴하다 install 통설치하다
remove 통치우다, 제거하다 frustrated 혱좌절한 artwork 몡예술 작품 sway 통흔들리다 blow 통(바람이) 불다 (blow-blew-blown)
finish 통마무리 짓다, 끝나다 <문제> engineer 몡공학자 climate 몡기후 aspect 몡특징, 양상 withstand 통견뎌내다

One day, Tim saw something astonishing while driving to work. The crosswalk was floating! He slowed down with caution and soon realized that it was just an illusion. ₃

This was a new type of crosswalk that was invented in a town in Iceland. The residents were afraid of fast-driving cars, so ⓐ special crosswalks were installed in the town. ₆ These crosswalks appeared to be 3D, but are actually *optical illusions. They are painted on a flat surface by using clever shading techniques that make ⓑ them look like white ₉ boards floating above the street!

These crosswalks are helpful in many ways. They're much cheaper than **speed bumps, but ⓒ they still increase drivers' ₁₂ _____. Pedestrians also love ⓓ them. From far away, people appear as if ⓔ they were walking on air. The crosswalks are now used in several other countries, ₁₅ including France, China, and Spain.

*optical illusion 착시 현상   **speed bump 과속방지턱

1 이 글의 제목으로 가장 적절한 것은?

① A Designer of 3D Crosswalks

② The Science of Optical Illusions

③ Drivers' Efforts to Make Road Safer

④ An Interesting Idea for Safety from Iceland

⑤ Types of Crosswalks Used in Different Countries

(서술형)

2 3D 횡단보도가 아이슬란드의 한 마을에 설치된 이유를 우리말로 쓰시오.

_____

3 이 글의 밑줄 친 ⓐ~ⓔ 중, 가리키는 대상이 나머지 넷과 <u>다른</u> 것은?

① ⓐ   ② ⓑ   ③ ⓒ   ④ ⓓ   ⑤ ⓔ

4 3D 횡단보도에 관한 이 글의 내용과 일치하면 T, 그렇지 않으면 F를 쓰시오.

(1) They are made of white boards that are printed in 3D. _____

(2) They could help save money compared to speed bumps. _____

(3) Other countries outside of Iceland use them today. _____

5 이 글의 빈칸에 들어갈 말을 글에서 찾아 쓰시오.

_____

Words

astonishing 휑 놀라운   crosswalk 몡 횡단보도   float 통 떠다니다   slow down 속도를 줄이다   caution 몡 경계(심)   illusion 몡 환상; 오해
Iceland 몡 아이슬란드   resident 몡 주민   appear 통 ~처럼 보이다; 나타나다   flat 휑 평평한   clever 휑 기발한, 재치 있는   shading 몡 명암
technique 몡 기법   board 몡 판자   pedestrian 몡 보행자   <문제> safety 몡 안전   compared to ~에 비해, ~과 비교하여
outside of ~ 외에, ~의 범위 밖으로

You go to a store, but all the shelves are empty. Where are all the goods? Actually, they were already bought by people who feared that the store would run out of supplies. ₃

Whenever there is a disaster, people tend to buy lots of products and store them. (a) This phenomenon is called panic buying. (b) In 2020, COVID-19 caused many people ₆ worldwide to be frightened. (c) They were scared of running out of supplies, so they bought enormous amounts of toilet paper, water, and canned food. (d) Canned food ₉ has become much cheaper recently. (e) Even with buying limits, products continued to sell faster than they could be supplied. ₁₂

Sometimes, panic buying can have harmful effects on society. It can cause prices of items like food and medicine to increase rapidly. Some people may not be able to get these necessities at all, which can put their lives in danger.

▲ 코로나 바이러스 위협으로 빈 육류 코너 선반　London | 2020.03.12

₁₅

₁₈

₂₁

Read & Learn

패닉 바잉은 순우리말로 '사재기', 그럼 독일어로는?
'사재기'를 독일어로는 'hamsterkäufe(햄스터코이퍼)'라고 하는데, 이는 '햄스터식 구매'라는 뜻이랍니다.
사재기의 양상이 햄스터가 먹이를 잔뜩 모아두는 것과 비슷하다는 점에서 착안한 말이라고 해요.

1 What is the best title for the passage?

① Stop Buying Things You Don't Use

② Fear of Disaster Causes People to Buy

③ Panic Buying Is Actually Good for Society

④ Disasters That Created Worldwide Panics

⑤ The Best Way to Prepare for Disastrous Situations

2 Among (a)~(e), which sentence does NOT fit in the context?

① (a)　　　② (b)　　　③ (c)　　　④ (d)　　　⑤ (e)

3 Complete each sentence with ONE word from the passage.

- Climate change will _____ extreme weather events such as floods and hurricanes.
- The police officers are trying to find out the _____ of the accident.

4 Choose the correct one based on the passage.

Panic buying occurs when people become (1) (frightened / depressed) during a disastrous situation. They buy (2) (more / less) than they need, and this can cause (3) (success / damage) to society.

Words

shelf 몝 선반　fear 동 두려워하다 몝 공포　run out of ~이 동나다, ~을 다 써버리다　supplies 몝 재고, 물자; (단수형) 공급, 보급
disaster 몝 재난 (disastrous 형 재난의; 처참한)　tend 동 경향이 있다　store 동 비축하다, 저장하다　phenomenon 몝 현상
panic 몝 패닉, 공황 (panic buying 패닉 바잉, 사재기)　cause 동 ~하게 만들다, 야기하다 몝 원인　frightened 형 겁에 질린　enormous 형 엄청난
toilet paper 화장지　canned food 통조림 식품　cheap 형 저렴한, 싼　limit 몝 제한, 한계　continue 동 계속하다, 계속되다
medicine 몝 약; 의학　rapidly 閉 빠르게　necessity 몝 필수품; 필요(성)　<문제> flood 몝 홍수　hurricane 몝 태풍, 폭풍　depressed 형 우울한

Review Test

정답 및 해설 p.89

1 단어의 성격이 나머지와 <u>다른</u> 것은?

① destroy   ② valley   ③ vary   ④ enjoy   ⑤ sway

2 짝지어진 단어의 관계가 나머지와 <u>다른</u> 것은?

① separate – separation   ② mix – mixture   ③ technique – technology

④ educate – education   ⑤ tend – tendency

[3-5] 다음 영영 풀이에 해당하는 단어를 보기에서 골라 뜻과 함께 쓰시오.

보기	route	shelf	suitable	enormous	fable

                                                          단어   뜻

3 a short traditional story that tells a lesson about life _____ _____

4 the path that you use to go from one place to another _____ _____

5 extremely large in size or amount _____ _____

[6-8] 다음 빈칸에 들어갈 단어를 보기에서 골라 쓰시오.

보기	phenomenon	pedestrian	symbol	illusion	caution

6 I almost hit a(n) _____ when I was riding my bike.

7 Lisa walked on the street with _____ because it was covered with snow.

8 The explorer thought he had found an oasis in the desert, but it was a(n) _____.

[9-10] 다음 밑줄 친 단어나 표현에 유의하여 각 문장의 해석을 쓰시오.

9 In many books and movies, the story <u>takes place</u> in the Middle East.

→ _____

10 Actually, they were already bought by people who feared that the store would <u>run out of</u> supplies.

→ _____

눈은 뱅글뱅글 머리는 빙글빙글

보이는 게 다가 아냐

착시는 우리 뇌가 착각을 일으켜 사물이 실제와 다르게 보이는 현상이에요.
지금부터 우리 눈을 의심케 할 신기한 착시 그림들을 소개할게요.
눈을 크게 뜨고 잘 보세요! 자, 준비됐나요?

그림 속 삼각형이 보인다?

그림에서 검은색 삼각형이 보이나요?
존재하지 않는 윤곽선은 왜 보이고, 그 가상의 삼각형은 왜 바탕색보다 더 까맣
게 보이는 걸까요?
이것은 우리 뇌가 전달받은 이미지에 직선을 채워 넣어서 생긴 착시 현상이에요.

가운데를 응시하다 보면 그림이 움직인다?

울렁울렁~ 나선형 모양이 움직이는 것처럼 입체적으로 보이지 않나요?
일반적인 평면이지만 사선 줄무늬 패턴이 결합하여 마치 빨려 들어가는 것 같은
착각을 일으키는 것이랍니다.

정말 나무만 보일까?

정말 나무만 보이나요? 관점을 다르게 해보세요.
나무가 아닌 배경에 집중하면 두 사람이 서로 마주 보는 그림이 보이게 돼요.
이렇게 뇌가 무엇을 먼저 보는지에 따라 같은 그림이라도 다르게 보일 수 있답
니다.

HackersBook.com

UNIT 09

Is your butt dead or alive? Try this to find out: Lie on the floor with your face down and lift one leg. See if your butt muscles become tight. If not, it may be a sign of Dead Butt Syndrome. 3

Your butt muscles connect to your hips and thighs, helping to support them. But if you spend too much of your 6 day sitting, your body (A) remembers / forgets to use your butt muscles. Instead, other body parts, like the waist, take over the responsibility of supporting your hips and thighs. 9 However, this can (B) prevent / cause hip pain, backache, and knee problems. It can even lead the hips and spine to rotate and twist. 12

How can you avoid this syndrome? The answer is rather simple. Don't sit still for too long! Get up and move your heels up and down at least every two hours. Doing this will 15 (C) weaken / strengthen your butt muscles.

Read & Learn

같은 듯 다른 "엉덩이"

a butt: 엉덩이
a butt은 엉덩이 두 짝 모두를 의미해요. 항상 단수형으로 써요.

hips: 엉덩이 쪽 고관절(골반)
hips는 정확히는 엉덩이 쪽 고관절, 즉 골반 부위를 의미해요. 주로 복수형으로 써요.

1 이 글에서 설명하는 죽은 엉덩이 증후군을 확인하는 자세로 가장 적절한 것은?

① ② ③ ④ ⑤

2 (A), (B), (C)의 각 네모 안에서 문맥에 알맞은 말로 가장 적절한 것은?

(A)		(B)		(C)
① remembers	......	prevent	......	strengthen
② remembers	......	prevent	......	weaken
③ forgets	......	prevent	......	strengthen
④ forgets	......	cause	......	weaken
⑤ forgets	......	cause	......	strengthen

3 엉덩이 근육이 약해질 경우 발생할 수 있는 일로 언급되지 <u>않은</u> 것을 <u>모두</u> 고르시오.

① 다른 신체 부위가 엉덩이 근육의 역할을 대신한다.

② 허리 근육이 이완되어 늘어난다.

③ 무릎에 문제가 생긴다.

④ 척추가 비틀어진다.

⑤ 허벅지 근육이 점점 약해진다.

(서술형)

4 다음 질문에 대한 답이 되도록 빈칸에 들어갈 말을 우리말로 쓰시오.

> Q. How can you prevent Dead Butt Syndrome?

A. 너무 오랫동안 앉아있지 말고, _____.

Words

butt 명 엉덩이 alive 형 살아있는 find out 알아내다 lie 동 눕다 lift 동 들다 muscle 명 근육 tight 형 단단한, 꽉 죄인 hip 명 골반 부위, 엉덩이
thigh 명 허벅지 support 동 지탱하다, 지지하다 waist 명 허리 take over 이어받다, 인수하다; 점령하다 responsibility 명 책임
backache 명 허리 통증 knee 명 무릎 rotate 동 돌아가다 twist 동 비틀어지다 rather 부 꽤 sit still 가만히 앉아있다 heel 명 발뒤꿈치
at least 최소한 weaken 동 약화하다 strengthen 동 강화하다

Have you ever tried spicy noodles with string cheese or milk with soda water? Interestingly, these combinations were created by consumers, and they became so popular that they were made into actual products. (①)

Usually, food products come with instructions to follow. (②) Coca-Cola With Coffee, for example, was first invented by people who enjoyed the scent of coffee and the sensation of soda. (③) Soon, the drink became very popular. (④) Then, the manufacturer took the recipe and used it to develop a new product. (⑤)

This trend does not just apply to food products. Some people combine two different perfumes to make a unique scent. Likewise, many consumers mix various goods like cosmetics, bathing products, or other daily necessities to match their preferences. Do you also have your own particular way of _____ products?

Read & Learn

너는 맛에 대한 계획이 다 있구나!
'커피 코카콜라'처럼 이색적인 조합으로 만들어진 대표적인 레시피 중 하나가 바로 '짜파구리'예요. 짜파구리는 짜파게티와 너구리를 섞어 만든 건데, 두 라면의 맛이 적절하게 어우러져 묘한 중독성을 지녔어요. 또한 영화 <기생충>에 등장한 이후 국내뿐만 아니라 전 세계에서 인기를 누리고 있죠! 해외에서는 너구리의 오동통한 면을 '우동'이라고 해서, 라면(Ramen)과 우동(Udon)을 합친 '람동(Ram-don)'이라는 이름으로 부른답니다.

1 이 글에서 설명하는 소비자의 유형으로 가장 적절한 것은?

① 모디슈머(modisumer): 자신만의 방법으로 제품을 재창조하는 소비자

② 프로슈머(prosumer): 제품의 기획이나 홍보에 적극적으로 참여하는 소비자

③ 체크슈머(checksumer): 제품의 성분과 재료 등을 꼼꼼하게 확인하는 소비자

④ 트윈슈머(twinsumer): 제품의 사용 후기와 의견을 참고하여 구매하는 소비자

⑤ 트라이슈머(trysumer): 새로운 서비스나 제품을 직접 체험해보고자 하는 소비자

2 이 글의 흐름으로 보아, 다음 문장이 들어가기에 가장 적절한 곳은?

But people sometimes choose to create their own recipes.

①   ②   ③   ④   ⑤

3 이 글의 빈칸에 들어갈 말로 가장 적절한 것은?

① using   ② buying   ③ testing

④ choosing   ⑤ reviewing

4 이 글의 내용으로 보아, 다음 빈칸에 들어갈 말을 보기 에서 골라 쓰시오.

보기   necessities   consumers   manufacturers   combinations

Many _____ mix items to create something entirely new.
Sometimes, these _____ become so popular that companies
release them as products.

Words

spicy 혱 매운 noodle 몡 면, 국수 string cheese 스트링 치즈(결을 따라 찢어서 먹을 수 있는 기다란 치즈) soda water 탄산수
combination 몡 조합 (combine 동 조합하다) consumer 몡 소비자 come with ~이 딸려 있다 instruction 몡 설명서 scent 몡 향
sensation 몡 느낌, 감각 manufacturer 몡 제조사 recipe 몡 조리법 perfume 몡 향수 likewise 부 마찬가지로 cosmetics 몡 화장품
bathing 몡 목욕 necessity 몡 필수품; 필요(성) preference 몡 기호, 선호 particular 혱 특별한, 특정한 <문제> review 동 검토하다
release 동 출시하다; 풀어주다

One day, a 10-year-old boy named Orlando Serrell was hit in the head by a ball while playing baseball. (①) He didn't go to the doctor because he only had a light headache. (②) He could suddenly perform *calendar calculations. (③) Given any date, he could immediately tell which day of the week it was or would be. (④) His answers were always correct. (⑤) In addition, he was able to remember every day perfectly after the accident. He knew what the weather was like, what clothes he was wearing, and every other detail of each day.

Later, the doctor said that he had developed **savant syndrome from the injury. Only a few people in the world have this syndrome, and they are usually born with it. It is rare to acquire savant syndrome later in life like Orlando. Therefore, doctors are now studying his mind to solve the mystery of _____.

*calendar calculation 달력에 관한 계산   **savant syndrome 서번트 증후군

Read & Learn **서번트 증후군이란?**

서번트 증후군은 자폐증이나 지적장애를 가진 사람이 특정 분야에서는 뛰어난 능력을 발휘하는 현상을 말해요. 음악, 미술, 암기 등 다양한 분야에서 그 재능이 나타날 수 있는데, Stephen Wiltshire라는 한 남성은 한 번 본 장면도 사진처럼 정확하게 그려내는 기억력과 그림 실력을 가졌어요. 20분 동안 도시 전역을 둘러보고 나면, 오로지 그 기억만으로 건물 하나하나까지 그대로 그릴 수 있다고 해요. 현재까지 그는 홍콩, 뉴욕, 런던 등 세계 각국의 도심 풍경을 그려왔답니다.

1 이 글의 제목으로 가장 적절한 것은?

① A Danger of Injuries in Sports

② How to Overcome Savant Syndrome

③ Loss of Memory after a Small Accident

④ People Who Are Born with Amazing Intelligence

⑤ An Unusual Ability That Was Accidentally Gained

2 이 글의 흐름으로 보아, 다음 문장이 들어가기에 가장 적절한 곳은?

> However, when the pain ended, something unusual happened.

①   ②   ③   ④   ⑤

3 이 글의 빈칸에 들어갈 말로 가장 적절한 것은?

① his endless pain   ② his creative thinking

③ his childhood memories   ④ his incredible ability

⑤ his survival of the accident

4 이 글의 내용과 일치하면 T, 그렇지 않으면 F를 쓰시오.

(1) Orlando Serrell은 머리를 다친 후 큰 수술을 받았다.   _____

(2) Orlando Serrell은 사고 이전의 기억을 잊어버리게 되었다.   _____

(3) 서번트 증후군을 후천적으로 갖게 되는 경우는 드물다.   _____

Words

headache 뗑 두통   calendar 뗑 달력   calculation 뗑 계산   immediately 튄 즉시   detail 뗑 세부 사항   develop 튕 생기다; 개발하다
injury 뗑 부상   acquire 튕 얻다, 습득하다   mind 뗑 정신   mystery 뗑 불가사의, 신비   <문제> overcome 튕 극복하다   loss 뗑 상실, 손실
amazing 뼹 놀라운   intelligence 뗑 지능   accidentally 튄 우연히   endless 뼹 끊임없는   childhood 뗑 어린 시절
incredible 뼹 놀라운, 믿을 수 없는   survival 뗑 생존

Did you know that the posters for the movie *Avengers: Endgame* are not the same in all countries? For example, the poster in China emphasized all of the characters equally by keeping them the same size. _____(A)_____, other countries' posters, including Korea's, had the most popular characters placed in the center and shown in a bigger size.

Likewise, there are different posters for *The Host, a Korean monster film, which was released in 202 foreign countries. In the original version of the poster, there was no monster. It only showed the main characters. _____(B)_____, the posters looked a lot different in other countries. Most of them portrayed the scene of a girl who was being grabbed by the tail of the monster.

In short, movie posters may vary in different countries. Their designs depend on what will draw a larger audience in each country.

*The Host 영화 〈괴물〉

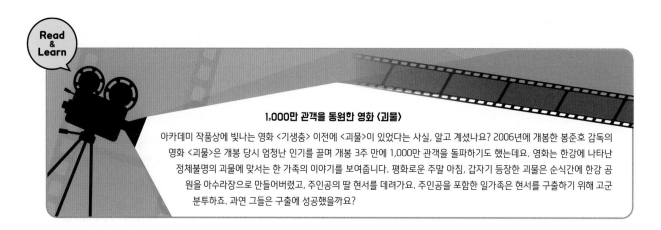

Read & Learn

1,000만 관객을 동원한 영화 〈괴물〉

아카데미 작품상에 빛나는 영화 〈기생충〉 이전에 〈괴물〉이 있었다는 사실, 알고 계셨나요? 2006년에 개봉한 봉준호 감독의 영화 〈괴물〉은 개봉 당시 엄청난 인기를 끌며 개봉 3주 만에 1,000만 관객을 돌파하기도 했는데요. 영화는 한강에 나타난 정체불명의 괴물에 맞서는 한 가족의 이야기를 보여줍니다. 평화로운 주말 아침, 갑자기 등장한 괴물은 순식간에 한강 공원을 아수라장으로 만들어버렸고, 주인공의 딸 현서를 데려가요. 주인공을 포함한 일가족은 현서를 구출하기 위해 고군분투하죠. 과연 그들은 구출에 성공했을까요?

1 What is the main topic of the passage?

① films with great posters

② why Korean films are popular globally

③ the importance of characters in movies

④ how movie posters vary between countries

⑤ movie preferences depending on the culture

2 Which is the best choice for both blanks (A) and (B)?

① Besides　　　② Therefore　　　③ However

④ For example　　　⑤ In other words

서술형 심화형

3 What is the reason for the underlined sentence? Write the answer in Korean.

_____

_____

4 Complete the table with words from the passage.

Characteristics of Korean Movie Posters

Avengers: Endgame	Only the famous characters were placed in the (1) _____ in a (2) _____ size.
The Host	It didn't include the (3) _____ and showed only the main characters.

Words

poster 명 포스터　avenger 명 복수하는 사람　emphasize 통 강조하다　equally 부 똑같이, 동일하게　release 통 개봉하다; 풀어주다
foreign 형 해외의, 외국의　original 형 원래의　portray 통 묘사하다　scene 명 장면　grab 통 붙잡다　tail 명 꼬리　vary 통 다르다
depend on ~에 달려있다　draw 통 끌어들이다　audience 명 관객

[1-3] 보기의 관계와 같도록 빈칸에 들어갈 단어를 쓰시오.

보기   calculation : calculate

1 _____ : survive

2 _____ : injure

3 _____ : combine

[4-5] 다음 영영 풀이에 해당하는 단어는?

4   to make something physically stronger or more effective

① strengthen   ② rotate   ③ access   ④ grab   ⑤ acquire

5   advice or information explaining how to do or use something

① intelligence   ② concentration   ③ instruction   ④ impression   ⑤ mystery

[6-8] 다음 빈칸에 들어갈 단어나 표현을 보기에서 골라 쓰시오.

보기   take over   overcome   waste   find out   emphasize

6   If you want to _____ some words in your presentation, say them louder.

7   As Ms. Flora will move to a different city, another teacher will _____ her classes.

8   Richard is trying to _____ a difficult situation without giving up.

[9-10] 다음 밑줄 친 단어나 표현에 유의하여 각 문장의 해석을 쓰시오.

9   Get up and move your heels up and down <u>at least</u> every two hours.

→ _____

10 Their designs <u>depend on</u> what will draw a larger audience in each country.

→ _____

How to Make a Soy Candle

콩에서 추출한 소이 왁스로 만든 소이 캔들은 냄새 제거에 탁월할 뿐만 아니라 심신안정과 숙면에도 도움이 돼요. 만드는 방법도 어렵지 않으니, 함께 만들어볼까요?

> **기본 재료:** 소이 왁스, 아로마 오일, 왁스를 녹일 냄비, 온도계, 향초를 담을 용기, 심지, 심지를 끼울 나무젓가락, 접착제

⚠️ **주의!** · 밀폐된 공간에서 오랫동안 향초를 켜면 건강에 좋지 않아요. 30분 정도 사용하면 충분하답니다. 사용 후에는 꼭 창문을 열어 환기해주세요.
· 불조심은 필수! 주변에 커튼 등 불이 옮겨붙을 수 있는 물건이 있는지 살펴보고, 외출하거나 잘 때는 꼭 불을 끄세요.

STEP 01 왁스 녹이기

왁스는 뜨거운 물에 중탕해서 녹여요. 가스레인지에 냄비를 올려 바로 녹이면 왁스에 불이 붙을 수 있으니 반드시 중탕하거나, 전자레인지에 약 3분 동안 돌려주세요. 왁스가 투명해지면 완전히 녹은 거랍니다.

STEP 02 아로마 오일 넣기

왁스 온도가 65~75도 사이의 적당한 온도가 되면 아로마 오일을 넣고 잘 저어주세요. 향초를 만들 때는 적정 온도를 지키는 것이 정말 중요해요. 온도가 너무 낮으면 잘 섞이지 않고, 너무 높으면 향기가 날아가 버리기 때문에 온도계가 꼭 필요하답니다.

STEP 03 향초 용기 준비하기

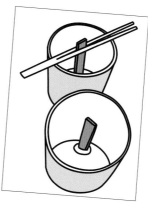

아로마 오일을 넣은 왁스가 알맞은 온도로 식는 동안 향초를 담을 용기를 준비해요. 심지를 알맞게 잘라 나무젓가락에 끼워주세요. 끼운 심지는 접착제로 용기 바닥에 붙여서 잘 고정해 줘요.

STEP 04 용기에 옮겨 담기

55~60도 정도로 식힌 왁스를 용기에 천천히 부어줘요. 천천히 부어야 굳었을 때 표면이 깔끔하고 고르게 나와요.

STEP 05 굳히기

이제 하루 정도 향초를 굳혀주기만 하면 끝! 완전히 굳기 전에 향초를 움직이면 표면이 울퉁불퉁해질 수 있으니 조심하세요.

HackersBook.com

UNIT 10

Every time you go to sleep, there is a chance that you will have a dream. (A) Sometimes you can even control what happens in a lucid dream. (B) But during a lucid dream, you know that you are dreaming. (C) When you dream, you usually don't realize you're dreaming until you wake up. For example, let's say you are dreaming that zombies are chasing you. Then you could change where you are just by thinking about it and escape.

Scientists say lucid dreams reduce anxiety and stress. This is because you can do anything you want in a lucid dream. These dreams are also known to boost creativity. Some artists have reported that they can try different artistic techniques in lucid dreams and then apply them in real life. However, frequent lucid dreams _____. They keep your mind awake, so you feel fatigued.

Read & Learn

자각몽을 꿀 때 나의 뇌는 어떨까?

자각몽을 꾸고 있는 사람의 뇌를 보면 일상적인 렘수면 상태와는 다른 모습을 볼 수 있어요. 우리가 자는 동안 뇌는 보통 비활성화되는데, 자각몽을 꿀 때는 전두엽의 일부분이 활성화되어 있는 것을 확인할 수 있거든요. 전두엽은 특히 인지 기능을 담당하기도 해서, 이 부위가 활동 중이라는 것은 곧 꿈을 꾸는 중에도 의식이 부분적으로 깨어있다는 것을 의미해요.

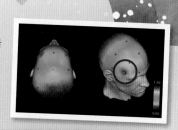

1 이 글의 주제로 가장 적절한 것은?

① how to avoid bad dreams

② why people dream while they sleep

③ various types and meanings of dreams

④ a dream that you recognize as a dream

⑤ a story behind the term of lucid dreaming

2 이 글의 문장 (A)~(C)를 순서에 맞게 배열한 것으로 가장 적절한 것은?

① (A) – (B) – (C)　　　② (B) – (A) – (C)　　　③ (B) – (C) – (A)

④ (C) – (A) – (B)　　　⑤ (C) – (B) – (A)

3 이 글의 빈칸에 들어갈 말로 가장 적절한 것은?

① keep you from waking up

② are not interesting anymore

③ are not good for your health

④ do not improve creativity

⑤ make you confuse dreams with reality

4 이 글의 내용으로 보아, 다음 빈칸에 들어갈 말을 글에서 찾아 쓰시오.

> While you are having a lucid dream, you know that you are dreaming and can sometimes ＿＿＿＿＿＿ what happens. According to scientists, lucid dreams can help ＿＿＿＿＿＿ anxiety and stress.

Words

chance 몡 가능성, 기회　lucid dream 자각몽　zombie 몡 좀비　chase 통 ~를 뒤쫓다　escape 통 탈출하다　anxiety 몡 불안
boost 통 신장시키다　report 통 보고하다　artistic 휑 예술적인　frequent 휑 잦은, 빈번한　awake 휑 깨어 있는　fatigued 휑 피로한
<문제> recognize 통 인식하다　term 몡 용어　reality 몡 현실

"Well, after a tough race, the candidate won by 287 votes. Congratulations to the chocolate chip cookie!"

Between 1992 and 2016, a cookie recipe competition 3 was held before every presidential election in the U.S. The competitors were the spouses of the presidential candidates. Each spouse submitted his or her own recipe. Then, citizens 6 voted for the one they liked more after baking the cookies themselves. Interestingly, the spouse of the winner usually won the presidential election as well. _____, 9 the Obamas, the Bushes, and the Clintons won both the cookie recipe contest and the presidential poll.

The competition was originally called the First Lady 12 Cookie Contest. However, when Hillary Clinton ran for president, her husband Bill had to submit his recipe. In response, (A) the contest's name was changed to the 15 Presidential Cookie Poll.

1 이 글의 제목으로 가장 적절한 것은?

① How the U.S. President is Selected

② Why People Should Participate in Voting

③ A Presidential Candidate Who Loved Cookies

④ The Best Cookies Always Have a Special Recipe

⑤ A Cookie Contest before the Presidential Election

2 이 글의 빈칸에 들어갈 말로 가장 적절한 것은?

① However   ② Instead   ③ Nevertheless

④ On the other hand   ⑤ For example

3 이 글을 읽고 Presidential Cookie Poll에 관해 답할 수 <u>없는</u> 질문을 <u>모두</u> 고르시오.

① Who was its last winner?

② When did it first start?

③ How was the winner decided?

④ What was its original name?

⑤ Who won it by the most votes?

(서술형)

4 이 글의 밑줄 친 (A)의 이유를 우리말로 쓰시오.

_____

_____

Words

tough 혱 힘겨운, 어려운 **race** 몡 경쟁, 경주 **candidate** 몡 후보(자) **win by** ~의 차이로 승리하다 **vote** 몡 표, 투표 동 투표하다
congratulation 몡 축하 **competition** 몡 경연, 경쟁 (**competitor** 몡 참가자, 경쟁자) **presidential** 혱 대통령의 **election** 몡 선거
spouse 몡 배우자 **submit** 동 제출하다 **citizen** 몡 시민 **bake** 동 굽다 **poll** 몡 선거, 여론 조사 **First Lady** 영부인 **run for** ~에 출마하다
in response 그에 따라, 대응하여 <문제> **select** 동 선정하다, 고르다 **participate in** ~에 참여하다 **nevertheless** 뷔 그럼에도 불구하고

▲ 우주선 Dragon호

The spacecraft Dragon came back to the Earth successfully again after its final mission in April 2020. It was the first spacecraft to make multiple trips to the International Space Station.

Usually, when spacecraft are sent into space, it's extremely difficult for them to return without damage. They must withstand temperatures of up to 1,850°C. Moreover, they don't always land in the right place. Heavy winds blowing in the upper atmosphere make it difficult to navigate to the landing zone. However, the Dragon succeeded in returning home without much damage. As a result, most of its parts were reusable, which saved the time and money needed to make new ones.

Spacecraft like the Dragon will eventually allow for more frequent and cheaper space travel. In fact, spacecraft developers are trying to make commercial space flight possible in the future. If they succeed, we might even take field trips to the Moon!

Read & Learn

HackersNEWS.com

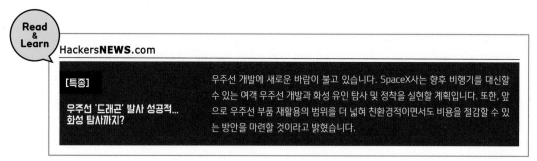

[특종]

우주선 '드래곤' 발사 성공적...
화성 탐사까지?

우주선 개발에 새로운 바람이 불고 있습니다. SpaceX사는 향후 비행기를 대신할 수 있는 여객 우주선 개발과 화성 유인 탐사 및 정착을 실현할 계획입니다. 또한, 앞으로 우주선 부품 재활용의 범위를 더 넓혀 친환경적이면서도 비용을 절감할 수 있는 방안을 마련할 것이라고 밝혔습니다.

1 이 글의 제목으로 가장 적절한 것은?

① Difficulties of Space Travel

② Building a New Space Station

③ A Big Project to Find a Lost Spacecraft

④ The First Spacecraft That Went into Space

⑤ A Spacecraft That Is Economical and Time-saving

(심화형)

2 우주선 Dragon호에 관한 이 글의 내용과 일치하지 <u>않는</u> 것은?

① It traveled to space multiple times.

② It was the first to visit the International Space Station.

③ It will help make space travel cheaper.

④ It didn't receive much damage while returning to the Earth.

⑤ Its parts could be used again for extra trips.

3 다음 빈칸에 공통으로 들어갈 단어를 글에서 찾아 쓰시오.

> • The city's _____ has been polluted by factories.
> • This restaurant has a romantic _____ .

4 이 글의 내용으로 보아, 다음 빈칸에 들어갈 말을 [보기]에서 골라 쓰시오.

> [보기]   return   commercial   multiple   recover

> When spacecraft _____ to the Earth, they easily get damaged. However, the spacecraft Dragon was capable of coming back safely and making _____ trips to space.

(Words)

spacecraft 몡우주선 (복수형: spacecraft) final 혱마지막의 mission 몡임무 multiple 혱다수의, 복수의 extremely 뷔극히
temperature 몡온도 up to 최고, ~까지 upper 혱상부의 atmosphere 몡대기, 공기; 분위기 navigate 동비행하다, 항해하다; 길을 찾다
succeed in ~에 성공하다 reusable 혱재사용할 수 있는 frequent 혱빈번한 developer 몡개발자 commercial 혱상업적인 flight 몡비행
field trip 견학 <문제> economical 혱경제적인, 알뜰한 time-saving 혱시간을 절약해 주는 pollute 동오염시키다 romantic 혱낭만적인
recover 동회복하다 be capable of ~할 수 있다

Minnie's brother Phil got a brand-new laptop. However, he would never let her use it. One day, Minnie tried to use his laptop while he was at soccer practice. But when she ③ turned ⓐ it on, it was locked with a password! Luckily, there was a clue to figure ⓑ it out:

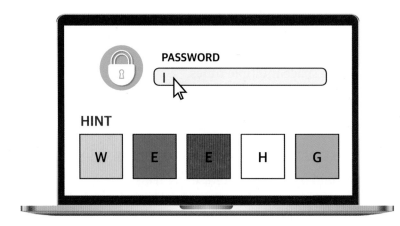

There were five colored boxes, and each box had a letter. ⑥ Minnie tried to enter these letters, but this didn't work. Only numbers could be entered. She thought about how the letters and colors were connected. The first box was yellow ⑨ and contained the letter *W*. After a few minutes, she smiled. She typed the numbers in and ⓒ they were right! (①)

Minnie started playing a computer game, but soon Phil ⑫ came home and caught her. (②) Surprisingly, he didn't say anything. (③) "Stop!" Minnie screamed as she watched him take a bite of it. (④) He was eating the donut ⑮ she had been saving all day! (⑤)

1 Write what ⓐ, ⓑ, and ⓒ refer to in the passage.

ⓐ: _____   ⓑ: _____   ⓒ: _____

2 Where is the best place for the sentence?

| Instead, he ran to the kitchen and grabbed a donut. |

①   ②   ③   ④   ⑤

3 Write Phil's laptop password.

PASSWORD: 6 _____ _____ _____ _____

4 How does Minnie feel by the end of the story?

① relieved   ② afraid   ③ upset

④ excited   ⑤ moved

5 Complete each sentence with ONE word from the passage.

- To use the phone, you have to _____ the password.
- People cannot _____ the museum after 8 p.m.

Words

brand-new 휑 최신형의, 완전히 새로운 **laptop** 뗑 노트북 (컴퓨터) **turn on** ~을 켜다 **lock** 동 잠그다 **password** 뗑 비밀번호
luckily 뷔 다행히 **clue** 뗑 단서, 힌트 **figure out** ~을 알아내다, 이해하다 **enter** 동 입력하다; 들어가다 **connect** 동 ~과 관련이 있다, 연결하다
type in ~을 입력하다 **catch** 동 발견하다; 잡다 (catch-caught-caught) **scream** 동 소리 지르다 **take a bite of** ~을 한 입 베어 물다
save 동 아껴두다, 남겨두다; 구하다 <문제> **grab** 동 집다, 붙잡다 **relieved** 휑 안도한 **moved** 휑 감동한

[1-2] 다음 영영 풀이에 해당하는 단어는?

1 to give a description or information about something to someone

① reschedule   ② catch   ③ distinguish   ④ improve   ⑤ report

2 related to buying and selling products

① chemical   ② commercial   ③ medical   ④ flexible   ⑤ professional

[3-4] 다음 괄호 안에서 알맞은 단어를 골라 표시하시오.

3 People's (anxiety / opportunity) is increasing because of the country's poor economy.

4 The detective found a (value / clue) that will help solve the crime.

[5-8] 다음 빈칸에 들어갈 단어나 표현을 보기 에서 골라 쓰시오. (단, 필요시 알맞은 형태로 고쳐 쓰시오.)

보기   submit   succeed in   win by   participate in   escape

5 I am sure that I will _____ getting a higher test score than last time.

6 The game was very exciting because the team _____ only one point.

7 Ms. Swift told the students to _____ their permission forms for the school trip.

8 Rolando _____ local volunteer activities last year to protect the animals.

[9-10] 다음 밑줄 친 단어나 표현에 유의하여 각 문장의 해석을 쓰시오.

9 <u>In response</u>, the contest's name was changed to the Presidential Cookie Poll.

→ _____

10 Minnie screamed as she watched him <u>take a bite of it</u>.

→ _____

Fun Fun 한 Break

드랍 더 비트

힙합의 소리를 찾아서…

"A Yo! 심장을 두드리는 비트, 나는 이 비트 위의 나그네!" 빠르게 쏟아내는 랩과 신나는 비트를 즐기다 보면
스트레스도 확 풀리기 마련인데요. 모두가 사랑하는 **장르인 힙합의 TMI**를 대방출합니다!

저 의외로 어려워요(?)

힙합의 역사는 의외로 짧아요. 1973년 미국 뉴욕의 브롱크스에서 처음 생겼거든요. 동네에서 디제잉을 하던 **DJ 쿨 허크(Kool Herc)**는 어느 날 여동생에게 파티에서 노래를 틀어달라는 부탁을 받았죠. 작은 동네 오락실에서 열린 파티였지만 그의 열정을 펼치기엔 충분했어요. 그는 사람들의 흥을 돋우기 위해 두 개의 턴테이블을 동시에 돌려 노래를 쉴 틈 없이 틀었어요. 덕분에 사람들은 끊김 없이 계속 춤을 출 수 있었죠. 이전에는 턴테이블을 한 개만 사용해서, 다음 노래를 틀 때면 정적이 흘러 흥이 깨지곤 했거든요. 그가 사용한 이 디제잉 기술이 점차 인기를 얻기 시작했고, 그가 사용한 비트 위에 빠르게 가사를 붙인 랩을 하기 시작하면서 힙합 장르가 탄생했답니다.

갑자기 분위기 "Drop it!"

힙합 노래를 듣다 보면 갑자기 래퍼가 "Drop it!"이라고 읊조리지 않나요? 갑자기 뭘 떨어트린다는 건지 어리둥절했다면 여길 주목하세요! 힙합 노래 중간중간 래퍼들은 즉흥적으로 추임새를 넣곤 하는데요. 많이 쓰는 추임새인 "Drop it!"은 "Drop the beat."를 짧게 말한 것으로, 우리나라 말로 하면 '비트 주세요.'의 느낌이랄까요? 또 많이 들을 수 있는 "Show me what you got."은 해석 그대로 '네가 가진 걸 보여줘', 즉 '너 랩 잘해? 그럼 내 앞에서 해봐.'라는 뉘앙스가 있어요. 랩 경연 프로그램의 배틀 장면이 생각나는 추임새죠?

Photo Credits

p.8   Wyss Institute at Harvard University

p.12   hkratky / Depositphotos.com

p.14   ChinaImages / Depositphotos.com

p.14   Marcos Mesa Sam Wordley / Shutterstock.com

p.14   "Mission Accomplished - ALS Ice Bucket Challenge" by Anthony Quintano / CC BY 2.0

p.26   Jasmien Smets & Kamp C

p.26   3D printed home (https://newstorycharity.org/wp-content/uploads/2019/12/3D_Feature.jpg)

p.41   Toywork / Shutterstock.com

p.46   Radish plants (https://www.nasa.gov/sites/default/files/thumbnails/image/iss064e013129.jpg)

p.48   "Baby Eyes" by Ali Moradmand / CC BY-SA 2.0

p.53   Morphart Creation / Shutterstock.com

p.56   "Duchamp: Marcel DUCHAMP, Fontaine, 1917" by Pablo Ibañez / CC BY 2.0

p.56   "Gold-colored Toilet" by stu_spivack / CC BY-SA 2.0

p.60   "James-Barry" / CC BY-SA 4.0

p.62   "Pandemic: Legacy" by Sean Hagen / CC BY-SA 2.0

p.72   Sweat Patch (https://internetofbusiness.com/wp-content/uploads/2018/03/sweatpatch-640x358.jpg)

p.94   Estate of Christo V. Javacheff

p.98   AlenaKr / Depositphotos.com

p.108   "el artista Stephen Wiltshire casi terminando el dibujo de la ciudad" by vladimix / CC BY-SA 2.0

p.116   Lucid Dreams (https://www.world-of-lucid-dreaming.com/image-files/lucid-dreams-found-to-occur-in-the-gamma-brainwave-frequency-range.jpg)

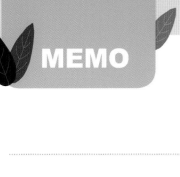

MEMO

MEMO

Smart, Skillful, and Fun Reading

HACKERS

READING SMART

LEVEL **3**

초판 7쇄 발행 2024년 12월 9일
초판 1쇄 발행 2021년 10월 1일

지은이	해커스 어학연구소
펴낸곳	㈜해커스 어학연구소
펴낸이	해커스 어학연구소 출판팀

주소	서울특별시 서초구 강남대로61길 23 ㈜해커스 어학연구소
고객센터	02-537-5000
교재 관련 문의	publishing@hackers.com
	해커스북 사이트(HackersBook.com) 고객센터 Q&A 게시판
동영상강의	star.Hackers.com

ISBN	978-89-6542-439-0 (53740)
Serial Number	01-07-01

중고등영어 1위,
해커스북 HackersBook.com

해커스북 중·고등

· 지문 전체를 담았다! 생생한 음성으로 리스닝도 연습할 수 있는 **지문 MP3**
· 교재 어휘를 언제 어디서나 들으면서 외우는 **미니 암기장 MP3**

한경비즈니스 선정 2020 한국품질만족도 교육(온·오프라인 중·고등영어) 부문 1위

최신 내신 기출
완벽 분석

전국 중학교 내신
기출 문제를 분석해
뽑아낸 문법 POINT 반영

중간/기말/서술형
실전문제

실제 시험에 나올 문제를
미리 풀어보며
내신 완벽 대비

풍부한 문제풀이
워크북

학습 내용의
충분한 반복 훈련으로
확실한 실력 향상

HACKERS
READING SMART
LEVEL **3**

해설집

HACKERS